THE POPE AND THE WORLD

THE POPE AND
THE WORLD

An Illustrated History of the
Ecumenical Councils

ANTON HENZE

Translated from the German by Maurice Michael

SIDGWICK AND JACKSON LTD

LONDON

1965

Originally published in Germany under the title of

DAS GROSSE KONZILIENBUCH by Anton Henze

Copyright © 1962 by Joseph Keller Verlag, Starnberg

Printed in Great Britain by
C. Tinling & Company Ltd
Liverpool, London and Prescot

CONTENTS

PLATES

The figures in the margins are the numbers of the
plates to which the text refers

NICAEA IN BITHYNIA

"THEN Constantine took counsel with himself. He considered all the circumstances and decided to strike another blow against the invisible enemy who had cast the Church into confusion. He convened the ecumenical council as a weapon on the side of God. He wrote respectfully to the bishops urging them to set out soon. He ordered the State posting service to convey the Council fathers or to put horses at their disposal. As meeting place he selected a very suitable one, that has its name from the goddess of victory, Nicaea in Bithynia."

Nicaea has now become Iznik, a village in Turkey, near the Sea of Marmora. Green hills give it its horizon on three sides, on the fourth is the shiny surface of Iznik Golü, Lake Iznik, blue-green with sunlight. At midday the village street was empty and hot. The Turkish coffee was bitter-sweet. What, I wondered, as I sat watching the peasants smoking their hubble-bubbles or gazing into the remoteness within them, would these men of Iznik say, if I read out to them that bit from Eusebius' biography of the Emperor Constantine describing the convening of the first Council of Nicaea? They would give me an uncomprehending look and then go back to their pipes or their contemplation. In their Iznik, time was standing still; it was neither in the twentieth century nor, indeed, in history. Their peasants' cottages, that surround a few buildings of the old Islamic town, are built on the ruins of Nicaea and are in a way older than the city of Nike, Greek goddess of victory. Antiquity, in which the succession of the years is of no account, and which has no recollection of what has gone before, is not confined to what came before the age of history, but also includes what can come after centuries of historical activity.

Out of the corn fields of Iznik rise the town walls of Nicaea. When the Goths made their incursion into Asia Minor in the year 260, they sacked the town. When they returned nine years later, they came up against an impregnable ring-wall, which Claudius Gothicus had had

1, 2, 3

built swiftly and in defiance of the ways of peace-time. Even grave-stones had been thankfully used to reinforce the brickwork. This polygonal wall was 5,536 yards long, 35 feet high and 13 to 25 feet thick. It was fortified with 108 towers and had four gateways. In the thirteenth century, when for a time Nicaea was capital of the Byzantine Empire, a second wall was built, lower than the first and from 14 to 20 yards from it.

It was through the gates of the inner wall of Nicaea that the Fathers of the First Council passed. The city that received them now lies beneath the fields and cottages of the peasants of Iznik, and it is only seldom that any ruins come to light. You will find ruins of the theatre between the South Gate and Water Gate; and to the north of the town are the ancient baths. Beyond the Istanbul Gate, and that no man's land of history that the abandoned ring-wall encompasses, lies the Field of Mars with a funeral pyramid standing there forlornly in the grass.

It is impossible to conjure up a picture of Nicaea at the time of the Councils. We do not even know where the emperor's summer palace stood, in which the Council was opened on May 20, 325.

"Once the invitations had gone out, one and all hastened there as though it were a race. They were lured by the hope of engaging in a good undertaking and of seeing that incomprehensible wonder, the person of such an Emperor", so Eusebius writes. Syrians and Cilicians, Arabs and Palestinians, a bishop from Persia and another from Spain, the chief servants of God from the churches of all Europe, Africa and Asia were assembled in the central hall of the palace, as the splendid figure of the Emperor walked in, and seated himself only at the invitation of the Council Fathers.

Eusebius describes Constantine in the terms and phrases that the Greeks and Romans reserved for their gods. What the emperor was really like in character and appearance is probably more accurately given by the sculptors who have portrayed him, though even they have been at pains to emphasize the power and authority of their subject. The best likeness of the Emperor is in the Capitol in Rome. It is an enormous head that stands on a column, on the front of which is a female figure representing a province of the Empire. To the left and right of the head are windows opening onto the inner court of the palace. Here and there, bits of other antique statuary stand against the wall, among them a giant foot and a cyclopean hand that are part of the enormous seated figure that the great head once topped. The Emperor's face retains its authority even in this surrealistic lumber room of history. Its aquiline nose juts out proudly; the chin has all the power of the general and ruler; the mouth tells of energy and determination; the eyes look out at the vastness of an empire that embraced the known world. This seated figure had its place in the Constantine basilica in the Forum, in the building of which, as well as in this statue, the Romans once again demonstrated their gift for conveying much with modest means, for being great in simplicity. They have lavished all the strength of their art on this statue of the Emperor, who deserted their city and raised Byzantium on the Bosphorus to the status of a second Rome.

"When the Lord turned again the captivity of Zion, we were like them that dream." The members of the Council must have thought of those words of the psalmist when Constantine appeared among them in the great hall at Nicaea. How things had changed! Here was the Emperor of Rome addressing an assembly of the Christian Church, kissing the wounds which his predecessor had inflicted on its bishops. But Constantine had not come to Nicaea just to honour the bishops and accept their homage. You have only to look at that head in the Capitol to know that this was a man who made big efforts only for big causes. He went to Nicaea hoping to cement the unity of the Empire. One year before, in 324, he had defeated the last of the joint emperors, Licinius, and was thus master of the whole empire. The Christian Church, to which he had granted freedom in the edict of Milan in 313, seemed to him a suitable instrument to unite this empire spiritually. Thus he was horrified when he learned that the Christians were far from agreed among themselves, and wrote to the theologians of Alexandria: "What wounds didn't my ear receive, still more my heart, when I was told of the division that had come about among you."

Strife over the doctrine of Arius had, indeed, split congregations and provinces. Arius, a priest in Alexandria, taught that Christ was a creation of the Father and not in himself eternal. His opponents saw Father, Son and Holy Ghost as manifestation of *one* God. Epiphanios, Arius' biographer, gives a rather unflattering description of him: "He was tall.

3

There was something obsequious about his manner. He sought by clever, adroit subterfuges to win every seeker over to his doctrine. He was flexible in association with others and knew the art of agreeing with all men." It is a pity that we have no portrait to correct this word picture, for there is no doubt that Arius was not as Epiphanios describes him. His writings show him to have been a strong, religious personality and a writer of class, and it cannot have been fortuitous that he had so many adherents.

Arius defended his views before the Council, but luck was not with him. His theory was rejected. On June 19, 325, the Council drew up in its place the Nicaean creed: "We believe in one God, the Almighty Father . . . and in one Lord Jesus Christ, the Son of God . . . God of God, Light of Light, true God of true God, engendered, not created, of equal nature with the Father". Arius was excluded from the congregation of the faithful and banished. Other questions that the Council debated were the date of the Easter festival and celibacy of the clergy, but the one great, enduring act of the Council was this creed. At the end, Constantine invited the Fathers to join him in celebrating his twenty years as emperor. He gave each a personal present and then dismissed them with the wish that peace should reign.

There is a strange fresco in the left nave of the church of San Martino ai Monti in Rome. It depicts Pope Silvester I enthroned under a baldachin. Seated on his right, but lower, is the Emperor Constantine, and on his left Saint Helena, the Emperor's mother. Round this little group bishops and prelates stand in a semicircle, and in the right foreground Arius and his adherents stand in chains, watching with unfathomable expressions some helmeted soldiers, who are burning their writings over a brazier. The picture, painted in the seventeenth century by an unknown artist, has a long legend telling that Pope Silvester held two synods in that church. At the second, which met in 325, he confirmed, in the presence of the Emperor and Saint Helena, the resolutions of the Council of Nicaea in Bithynia. "Because of his age, the bishop had not come from the imperial city of Rome," Eusebius wrote in his biography of Constantine, "but he sent priests to represent him."

This belated honouring of the Council of Nicaea must have been painted *after* the Council of Trent (1545–1563). A picture of a session of the latter's General Congregation, which met in the church of Santa

Maria Maggiore, still hangs in that church. Venetian engravers,
Europe's main news-commentators in the sixteenth century, simplified
it and made countless copies of it. Evidently, one of these came into the
hands of the painter of the murals in San Martino ai Monti, who without scruple transformed it into a picture of the Council of Nicaea. This
was quite in accordance with the custom of the day, for people had not
yet got the idea that historical events and people should be depicted in
the settings and garments in which they had appeared. Thus, the painter
has depicted Pope and Emperor in as free and easy a relationship as
they might have had in the Rome of his own day; but at the synod of
325, Constantine most certainly did not sit at the feet of the Pope. It
was the Emperor who summoned the Council and synod, and he was
its dominant personality. We know now from church documents that
he did not even seek the Pope's agreement when planning the Council.
This picture of the Council is surprising not only in copying that of
Trent and being so unhistorical, but also in its peculiar composition. In
accordance with the strange tenets of Mannerism, the style that
dominated European art from 1520 to about 1600, the incidental is
shoved into the foreground; on the left of the picture the guards are
very much in evidence with their halberds and on the right the burning
of Arius' books attracts far more attention than is its due, while the
important people, the Emperor and Pope, and even the Holy Writ
lying on a lectern, have been thrust to one side. The middle is empty,
while the really important thing is taking place away in the background, where the Holy Ghost is illuminating the hearts of the Council
Fathers.

This painting makes legend of history. There are other portraits of
Constantine and documents that allow us to correct the historical image
of the Emperor, but this is not possible with the Pope of the first
Ecumenical Council. Silvester I is pure legend, in both picture and
word. Undoubtedly the Council of Nicaea recognized the authority of
the Pope before the entire world, but the legend of Silvester's doings
and of his relationship to Constantine cannot pass any historical
test.

In the thirteenth century, the walls of a chapel in the monastery of
the Quattro Coronati in Rome were painted with murals depicting the
Silvester legend. They show Constantine, still a heathen, attacked by

5

leprosy. The priests of the heathen deities in Rome advise him to bathe in the blood of innocent infants. Then Saint Peter and Saint Paul appear to him in a dream, and they tell him that he can find a cure on Mount Soracte. There the Emperor's messengers find the exiled Pope Silvester. He gives them pictures of the Apostles, and Constantine is miraculously cured by these. Filled with gratitude, Constantine conducts the Pope to Rome, himself leading the Pope's horse by the bridle. Then, while the imperial nobles look on from the towers of the eternal city, he presents the Pope with the tiara. We are eyewitnesses of the gift of Constantine, the legend according to which the Emperor Constantine, made Pope Silvester a gift of the city of Rome, thereby laying the foundation for the papal state of the future.

The heads, gestures and garments, the style and colours of the painting are Byzantine, but the intention is purely Roman. Since the start of their history, the Romans have never been able to keep religion and politics apart; and when Rinaldo Conti, Cardinal of Ostia, commissioned the murals, the intention was not merely to honour the holy Silvester, there was a political purpose as well. That was the year 1246. Since the Council of Lyon in the previous year, the struggle between Pope Innocent IV and Emperor Frederick II for temporal power had assumed apocalyptic proportions. Now Cardinal Conti, a friend of the Pope, was taking a hand in his own way, making "history" speak in pictures, which informed the people of Rome that no less a personage than the Emperor Constantine had presented the Pope with the temporal sword. If that was the case, must not Frederick really be the beast of the Apocalypse even to think of disputing it?

While decadent Rome was seeking to bolster itself up with legends, Nicaea in Bithynia had become the summer residence of the Emperors, who since Constantine's day had resided in Constantinople, the second Rome. Then, some 450 years after the first ecumenical council of the Christian church, the city was buzzing with the debates of a second council, the seventh assembly of the church.

In August 766, sixteen death sentences had shocked the people of Constantinople. Those condemned and swiftly executed were all officers of the imperial guard or high officials. What crime had they committed? The police had found icons in their homes, images of Christ, of the Mother of God and of the saints! Reading that, one feels that one must have got one's history wrong: was Constantinople then already in the hands of the Mohammedans? By no means. The ruler of the Bosporus was that very Christian emperor, Constantine V. The trouble really began in 726, when Emperor Leo III ordered the removal of all icons from the churches and palaces; this was followed in 720 by another edict ordering their destruction. Leo, and the other enemies of sacred pictures, the iconoclasts, triumphed; but the other side, the iconodules would not accept defeat. They took to the barricades, fell fighting for their pictures, died beneath the executioner's sword or in exile. Artists who painted new icons had their right hands cut off, monasteries and nunneries were turned into barracks and granaries if the monks and nuns refused to stop venerating images. These iconoclasts invoked the Old Testament's prohibition of images and saw confirmation of their ideas in Islam's complete lack of them. Leo III's edict ordering the destruction of all images, explained that, since it was impossible to depict the divine nature of Christ, any representation of him could only depict him as a human; to do that, however, was heretical.

There were, of course, political motives behind their theological argument. In ancient Rome the image of the Emperor had had vicarious power. If the Emperor was unable himself to be present, he sent his image and that acted for him, was his representative. It had retained this function even after .he emperors became Christians and regarded themselves as the representatives of Christ on earth. As the saints became venerated more and more, it was not long before their pictures were beginning to compete with the Emperor and his image.

The question then arose: who represented Christ on earth, the Emperor and his image or the saints and theirs? The people of Byzantium decided in favour of the saints, and this seemed dangerous to the Emperor. He had only just been able to defeat the attacking Arabs before the very gates of Constantinople and, if he was to continue to stand up to the Arab attack, he needed complete secular and temporal power. The ban on sacred pictures was to him a political and, in the last resort, also a religious necessity. What help would icons be to the people of Byzantium, if the empire and its cities fell into the hands of the Mohammedans?

In the fields of Iznik are the ruins of the Christian city of Nicaea,

6 which ceased to exist in 1330, when it was captured by Sultan Orhan. It is mentioned one hundred and sixty years later, in Hartmann Schedel's history of the world (1492), and his illustrators seem to have been most impressed by the city walls and the round-arched gateways between their rectangular and polygonal towers. They show the waters of Lake Iznik lapping against the masonry of the walls, and above the roofs rises the cupola of a church, presumably the Koimessis Panagias, holding aloft a crescent, not a cross. The ruins of this church, which now lie to the south-east of the village, prove that it was indeed a cupola-basilica. We don't know when it was built; but its plan suggests the eighth or ninth century. It is possible that the Council Fathers of 787 prayed in it; but it was not the official church of the Council. That honour belonged to the Hagia Sophia, the ruins of which stand on the western fringe of the village; though it was long thought that the other three-naved church, in whose unvaulted middle nave trees and bushes grow, was the one. Excavations carried out by A. M. Schneider in 1936 proved that this was not the case. The walls are those of a mosque built by the architect Sinan in the seventeenth century on the foundations of a Christian church that had been burned to the ground, but which must have originated after 1065, in which year Nicaea was devastated by an earthquake. The Hagia Sophia, built by the Emperor Justinian (527–565) also collapsed. This was the church of the 787 Council. Schneider found its foundations, from which you can see that it had the three-nave construction. Here and there among the foundations there were still bits of its mosaic floor. Subsequent structures retained the apse, in which the early Christian arrangements of seats is represented. The bishop's seat rises up from the apex of this semi-circular vaulted space, flanked on either side by six rows of seats for the priests and deacons.

The bishop's seat and the wall-benches are still to be seen as naked brick; but when the great ones of the Second Council of Nicaea took their places on them on September 24, 787, they were, like the whole church, faced with shining marble. In 780, the Empress Irene became regent in Byzantium, as her son, Crown Prince Constantine, was still a minor. She belonged to the iconodules, and at a synod over which she presided, held in the Church of the Apostle in Constantinople, the question of raising the ban on pictures and images was mooted. When it looked as though the ban was going to be raised, the imperial guard forced its way into the church with drawn swords and drove the Fathers out. In Nicaea, however, the iconodules were more fortunate., Some 300 bishops, among them two legates of Pope Hadrian I (772–795) arrived for the Council. The discussions continued until October 23, but they quickly decided in favour of icons, basing their decision on the magnificent theology of images formulated by Johannes of Damascus (675–749). The Council proclaimed the dogma that images of Christ, the Mother of God, angels and the saints are permissible, because by them the beholder is encouraged to remember the person portrayed and to strive to imitate him. Whoever revered a picture of Christ in this way, paid homage to Christ and not to the picture as such. A distinction must be made, however, between veneration and worship, the latter being due to God alone. Theophanes, historian of the second Council of Nicaea, commenting on this, wrote: "There was nothing new in this decision. It merely preserved the doctrine of the holy Father and rejected the new false doctrine. Now peace could reign in God's Church. The enemy, however, did not cease to strew weeds through his accomplices."

These accomplices were at work in Byzantium, where the Nicaean resolution was not finally put into force until 843, and one of them was Charlemagne. The resolutions of the Second Council of Nicaea were drawn up in Greek. In the West a translation was published that was incorrect, for it omitted the distinction between veneration of pictures and worship of God that had been so specifically made in Nicaea. Charlemagne, who even before his coronation in Rome in 800 had set up as protector of the church and legal heir in the West of the Emperor Constantine, convened a synod that met in Frankfurt in 794 in opposition to the Council of Nicaea. Charlemagne thought more of relics than of pictures and images, and so the synod resolved that the doctrine of the Second Council of Nicaea was not universally binding and it called upon Pope Hadrian I to excommunicate the Emperor of Byzantium. Hadrian refused to recognize the Frankfurt resolutions. The iconodules who had won at Nicaea now triumphed in the West as well. This led to the merging at the Court of Charlemagne in Aachen of the Germanic spirit and Roman-Byzantine idea of man, which was to form the basis of European art. In Charlemagne's copy of the Gospels, now in the

British Museum, Saint John the Evangelist is depicted sitting with the air of a Roman senator in a room reminiscent of the imperial palace at Constantinople. In this and other paintings in books, the anonymous artists have used Roman and Byzantine models. They have not merely imitated, but also created afresh from other people's material. This was a decision that has made world history, in that it introduced the human image into western art, thus giving painters and sculptors a theme that they have not exhausted in a thousand years.

At the time of the First Council, the Lake at Iznik was still a bay of the open sea and accessible to shipping. As I left the village, the great sun of Anatolia was setting over the lake. Soon the ring-walls of Nicaea, far too vast for Iznik, lay behind us. As night fell, I could not help thinking how, though archaeologists go to the farthest corners of the earth to excavate sunken cities and lost civilizations, the one decisive event in the history of western art and the place where it was enacted at the Second Ecumenical Council, Nicaea in Bithynia, seem to be for-gotten. We tend to regard all that as a matter of course, forgetting that the outcome might have been so very different. It was touch and go that the Fathers at Nicaea did not vote *against* pictures and images. If they had, the West would have been without paintings as the world of Islam is, where, apart from architecture, there is only non-figurative ornamentation. The paintings and statues in which we of the West have honoured our saints and great men and lovely women would never have been made. It is as inconceivable that painters and sculptors have not joined forces and erected a monument to Nicaea on the fields of Iznik, as it is that art historians and archaeologists have not yet excavated Nicaea, the place where the life and death of western pictorial art was decided.

CONSTANTINOPLE

THE imposing circus that Emperor Theodosius I (379–395) *13* presented to his capital, Constantinople, suffered all the historical ups and downs that thereafter beset that city on the Golden Horn. It stood near where the Blue Mosque now stands, and the site is still marked by the obelisk that, in 390, the Emperor set up as a *10* memorial to himself. The obelisk had been made on the orders of Thotmosis III of Egypt (1504–1450 B.C.), and Theodosius only provided it with a new pedestal, which his Byzantine sculptors carved with reliefs. On the south-eastern side of the pedestal the Emperor is shown in the midst of his suite attending the chariot races that were held in the circus. He is standing between his sons in the imperial box, holding in his right hand the laurel wreath with which he is going to crown the winner. The marble has not been able to withstand the destructive forces of the climate, and his face and figure are weathered.

You get a better picture of the Emperor from his coins, and there is, *11* too, a missorium, one of those pictures of himself that he sent to the provinces to act as his pictorial deputy, which provides a magnificent picture of him. It was found in Spain, a round silver disc, thirty inches in diameter, in the middle of which Theodosius sits enthroned. His face has all the strength and vigour of a general of the Roman Army. The fact of his being a Christian seems to have softened somewhat the severity of his features. Round his tonsure he wears the diadem of pearls that the emperors had worn ever since the days of Constantine I. His head is emphasized by a ring of light, corresponding to the green glory, the nimbus that in Byzantine painting was accorded to emperors and popes during their lifetime, dead ones having a golden halo. The robe of a Roman consul falls loosely from the Emperor's shoulder to his knee. He is sitting in front of the "tribune", the pillared stand with three compartments, that in Rome provided the setting for the exercise of power by judges and emperors. His attitude is that in which Christ was depicted; so that Christ's deputy on earth resembles his heavenly master even in posture.

Theodosius I, a Spaniard, was Emperor at the time of the First Council of Constantinople, the second general assembly of the Church. The peace that Constantine the Great had wished the Church, when he said farewell to the Fathers attending the first council at Nicaea, had not lasted long. In fact, the Emperor himself destroyed it. At Nicaea, Constantine banned Arius and his doctrine; yet at the end of his life he accepted Arian baptism. The Arians thus won power at Court and throughout the empire. As Saint Jerome later described it: "The world gave a sigh and noticed with amazement that it had become Arian." Theodosius, however, had no truck with the Arians. "We wish that all people that enjoy the clemency of our rule shall live in the faith that the Apostle Peter handed down to the Romans . . . . In accordance with the exhortation of the apostle and the teaching of the evangelists we hold to be true that Father, Son and Holy Ghost are one deity in equal majesty and holy trinity." So he proclaimed on February 27, 380. Having entered Constantinople in triumph, he deposed the Arian bishop, Macedonius, and appointed Gregory of Nazianzus the new chief shepherd. The church historian Socrates relates how he then "without delay summoned a synod of the Church in order to establish the creed of Nicaea."

The Council met in May 381 in the imperial palace at Constantinople. This stood somewhere between the Hagia Sophia and the Blue Mosque, which was put up at the beginning of the seventeenth century. In 1918 and 1919 Theodor Wiegand, the archaeologist, established the precincts of seven palaces; but as no more than the foundations had been preserved, these were covered up again. However, one can still see the remains of the Holy Palace in which the Emperor lived. Today, these comprise the Mosaic Museum, which stands beside the Blue Mosque, where too is the obelisk of Emperor Theodosius. In the ruins of one of the forecourts there is a mosaic floor depicting scenes of everyday life: children playing, domestic animals being cared for, hunters hunting. The colours glow deep in their white ground, people and animals and Nature vie for one's attention. One would like to think that the Council fathers trod this floor in 381, for otherwise there are so few traces of the Council left, but this is not the case: the mosaic is sixth-century work.

Gregory of Nazianzus presided over the Council. He came from Cappadocia in Asia Minor, the country which provided the back-woodsmen of the world of antiquity. He had studied philosophy in Athens and had then adopted the life of a hermit, only ascending the bishop's throne in Constantinople with reluctance. Ironically, he wrote of himself: "My ragged appearance is not a recommendation and you could scarcely call me handsome." But there is nothing of the ragamuffin about him in the oldest picture of him we have, nor any *15* sign of the cares of the bishop and Council father. This is a mural in Santa Maria Antiqua in the Forum in Rome, in which Gregory figures as one of a long row of fathers of the eastern Church, all depicted front view and identified by inscriptions in Greek. These murals were the work of painters of Byzantine origin and executed on the orders of Pope Paul I (757–767). Time, however, has dealt hardly with them. Many are almost effaced, others have only one eye left or a gesturing hand. Gregory is standing to the right of his student friend and companion-in-arms in the fight against the Arians, Saint Basil, and, indeed, has fared better than his neighbour in the Lord. His face has been preserved. It is a long face, framed by the uncut beard of the hermit. The nose is masterful and dominant like a mountain ridge in Cappadocia; and his big eyes blaze with the dark fire of the Byzantine icons. The forehead is round, high and clean. It is the face of a saintly poet that looks out at you from the dim distance of history. These later painters from Byzantium have given their great countrymen a striking memorial, for Saint Gregory was in fact a poet. The fine ladies and snobs of Constantinople might turn up their noses at his clothes, but they fought to get in and hear him preach.

A man with this nature was not the right one to deal with the complicated business and squabbling of the Council. When, after the arrival of the Egyptian bishops, all the energies of the Council were taken up in the petty quarrel over the Bishop of Antioch, Gregory resigned from both bishopric and presidency. The sermon he preached then in Constantinople is one of the most beautiful farewells in literature:

"Farewell, my great city that loves the Lord. Stride on towards the truth. Reform yourself and fear God. There is nothing disgraceful in changing, but to persist in evil, is to injure oneself. Farewell, East and West, for whom and by whom I have been attacked. Few only will approve my withdrawal. But consider: he who steps down from a throne, not only loses something. He also attains a seat that is much higher and more secure than the one he has lost.

"But above all, and always, my cry is: farewell, you angels, guardians of this church, you who saw my arrival and are witnessing my departure. May the hand of God guide our fates. Farewell, most holy Trinity, you who are my grief and also my adornment. Let me not have been wasted. Rescue this, my people. For they are my people, even if another is in charge of them. Oh, may you be able always to tell me that progress is being made, that you are growing in word and deed. Do you, my children, observe my bequest."

We have no picture of Saint Gregory's successor to the presidency of the Council. He was a lawyer called Nectarius and came from Tarsus. He even had to be baptized before he could preside over the Council, but he did a good job. The Council made progress and achieved its ends. The status of the see of Constantinople was agreed: it was to come immediately after Rome. But above all the Council attested the divinity of the Holy Ghost. The Arians maintained that the Holy Ghost was a creature of the second person in God, the Son. The Council fathers, however, reaffirmed and supplemented the creed formulated at Nicaea. They promulgated the Creed of Nicaea and Constantinople, on which all Christianity has been agreed ever since. On the question of the Holy Ghost, the Nicaean Creed says: "And I believe in the Holy Ghost, the Lord and Giver of life, who proceedeth from the Father and the Son, who with the Father and the Son together is worshipped and glorified, who spake by the prophets. . . ." The Trinity, "the grief and adornment of Saint Gregory of Nazianzus, triumphed at his Council.

The mosaics in the church of San Vitale in Ravenna mirror for us mortals the glories of Heaven. Christ and the saints there fill the walls and vaulted ceiling. Where they are, the Emperor too has his place. In San Vitale, he is not alone; but the Empress, who claims equal rights, is there with him. When San Vitale was being built, Justinian I (527–565) was Emperor in Constantinople. His wife was called Theodora, and she is depicted here, dominating the left-hand wall of the apse. The Emperor usually presented newly built churches with a chalice and other liturgical vessels and appliances, and this custom is depicted in paint for the first time in San Vitale, where the Empress Theodora is

15

shown holding the golden chalice. She is wearing a wide, flowing violet cloak and a costly diadem of pearls glows in her black hair. Her narrow, wilful face is framed by pendants, and there is an aureole to show her imperial rank. She is shown standing in a shell-niche to emphasize her separate entity as Empress. Ladies-in-waiting accompany her, as she makes her way to the church, and they have halted for a moment and their eyes, like those of their mistress, are turned on the beholder without seeing him. Then they move on in solemn procession. A servant pulls back the curtain over the church door: the way to the altar is free.

Sixth-century art did not set out to tell stories or relate court gossip. It exalted people, disregarding what in them was all too mortal and lending permanence to their fleeting presence. "But what remains, is the work of poets." Hölderin's expression applies equally well to the painters of the sixth century. Theodora and her suite live on in surroundings in which heaven and earth are balanced. These are lit by colour: velvety green, the red of purple, the black of melancholy and the comfort of gold. Looking at this picture, what does it matter that Theodora was the daughter of a Syrian bear-leader? One is no longer interested in the anecdotes of Procopius and his disclosures about the early life of Theodora the actress. The road to power was as strange and incomprehensible in the sixth century, as it is today. Then, as now, God gave the brains to go with the office. Procopius says in his *Secret History* that Theodora had a lot of influence over the Emperor. It was not only in politics that she had views of her own, but in religion too. Here Theodora went her own way: she was a Monophysite.

The Council of Chalcedon (451) had unanimously accepted "one and the same Son, Our Lord Jesus Christ, complete as deity, complete as man." According to its decision, the two natures of Christ, the divine and the human, merged "unmixed and unchanged, not separate and not isolated, both in one person". The Monophysites, however, continued to believe that Christ inhabited his body only as though it were a temple, that his divinity could be separated from his humanity. The Emperor Justinian, concerned for the unity of his empire, tried at the Second Council of Constantinople (533–554) to reconcile the Monophysites to the Chalcedon pronouncement. He met them to the extent that he had the writings of the theologians of Antioch, the most violent opponents of monophysitism, condemned. The Council accepted his argument and after some initial opposition the Pope, Vigilius, also agreed to it.

The Fatih mosque now stands where the Second Council of Constantinople held its sessions. Sultan Mehmed II had it built between 1463–1470, and it was restored in the eighteenth century. Beside the inner portal you can read the prophetic words told the sultan by Mohammed: "You will conquer Constantinople. What good fortune for the army that succeeds in this, what good fortune for its commander!" Mehmed II was in command of the fortunate army which, in May 1453, stormed the new Rome, Constantinople. By building this mosque, Mehmed captured the eastern capital of Christianity a second time. For its site he chose that of the Church of the Apostles, which he pulled down. This was not just one of the many houses of God that dotted Constantinople. Early Christian art had expended all its inventiveness and sense of form on it. Constantine had built his own mausoleum beside it, and later Emperors followed his example. This Church of the Apostles served their successors in Byzantium as episcopal church. The person who pulled it down and replaced it by a mosque was thus twice a *fatih*, i.e. conqueror. We know that this Church of the Apostles, which Constantine had had built on the fourth of the hills of the new Rome and which his successors had several times restored, was one of the great domed basilicas, and that Eulalios furnished it with mosaics that made him famous as, perhaps, the greatest master of early Christian art. But there is no trace of any of it left. If you have seen Saint Mark's in Venice and admired its five domes, you have seen a pale image of the other's glories.

Of Justinian, Procopius said: "He never spoke the truth to those with whom he conversed. Although he was himself artful in word and deed, he was at the mercy of anyone who wished to cheat him," and at the Council of Constantinople he seems to have cheated himself, for what appeared as a triumph for the Emperor was nothing of the kind. The Monophysites persisted in their beliefs, and condemnation of the Antioch school did not in any way impair the creed pronounced at Chalcedon, as Pope Vigilius had realized.

As so often happens, we here see the painter trying to correct the historian, in this case in his picture of Justinian's personality. The 16 Justinian who looks out at us from the wall of the apse of San Vitale in

1

2

QUESTO SAGROSANTO LVOGO, CELEBRI UNA VOLTA TERME DI TITO, DOMIZIANO, E TRAJANO IMPE
SONO STATI DA S. SILVESTRO PP. CELEBRATI DUE CONCILJ. IL PRIMO, L' ANNO DEL SIGNORE CC
INTERVENTO DI COSTANTINO MAGNO, DI S. ELENA, DI CALFVRNO PISONE PREFETTO DI ROMA, DI
CLERO ROMANO, E DI CCLXXXIV VESCOVI. IL SECONDO, L' ANNO CCCXXV, COLL' ASSISTENZA D
COSTANTINO, E COLL' INTERVENTO DI CCXXV VESCOVI. ED IVI FVRONO CONFERMATI, GLI ATT
IO DI NICEA IN BITINIA, FURONO CONDANNATI ARIO, SABELLIO, VITTORINO, ED ABBRUCIATI

8

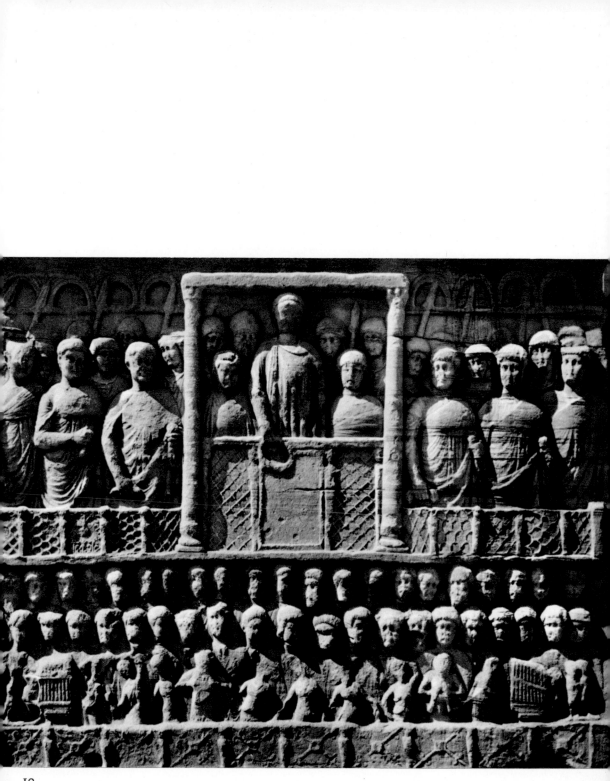

12

18

Ravenna does not look at all like Procopius' "simple-minded rogue". It is a face full of harmony, with a fine straight nose, and a small but strong mouth that reveals that he also knew what pain was. There is a *17* firm but melancholy look in the eyes beneath the dark curves of the wide-arched brows. You do not need the diadem of pearls and precious stones and the purple cloak to know that here is a man of authority. Being who he is, he has stepped forward from his suite and is about to present the church with a great golden paten. He is ready to share first place with Maximiamus, Bishop of Ravenna. You can believe that this Justinian revered the state, codified the laws and restored their authority, and that it was his pious endeavour to bring untiy of faith back to the Christian world. This mosaic picture and its colour give a different complexion to the Second Council of Constantinople. What at first sight appeared as self-deception on the Emperor's part, now proves to have been the tragedy of failure, and we can understand this, when we remember that the division, the divergence of belief, began at the top, being there in the Emperor's own marriage. It is not only in San Vitale that Justinian and Theodora stand on different sides of the church.

The unity that Justinian, who was strong, was unable to compel, fell into the lap of a weaker successor, Constantine IV. When he held the Third Council of Constantinople, the sixth ecumenical council of Christianity, Alexandria and Jerusalem, the two strongholds of Monophysites, were already in the hands of the Arabs. From November 7, 680, till September 16, 687, the Council Fathers debated and discussed in the domed hall of the imperial palace, but the outcome was really never in doubt. The Council was presided over by a legate sent by Pope Agathon from Rome and it re-enacted the dogma of the five preceding councils. The Monotheletes and their spokesman were condemned as heretics.

The event is depicted in an illuminated manuscript of about A.D. 1000 that belonged to the Emperor Basil II and is today the property of the Vatican Library. The Emperor is sitting in an apse with the chief *19* Council Fathers. Out of their midst rises the patriarchal cross with its two bars, before which a Monothelete has prostrated himself. Each Council Father holds a book in his hands to show they are Fathers of the Church. They and the Emperor have haloes, giving a large background to their heads.

Historically, the most interesting personality of the Council was that of a dead man, Pope Honorius I. He was one of the heretics they condemned. Sergius, Patriarch of Constantinople (610–638), had tried in his own way to reconcile monophysitism with the imperial church. He attributed to Christ only the natural energy and will of God made flesh. Honorius, to whom the hair-splitting of the eastern theologians was quite foreign, let himself be deceived by this and concurred with it. In 638, it was declared binding in an imperial decree. Monophysitism, the doctrine of Christ having one nature, was thus replaced by monotheletism, the doctrine of one will. This "Honorius question" has remained topical ever since the days of this Third Council of Constantinople and greatly troubled the First Vatican Council in 1870. The question was: Was Honorius condemned as an adherent of the heresy of monotheletism or for heedlessness? An answer had already been given by Pope Leo II (682–683), who, although he acknowledged the Third Council of Constantiople, had removed Honorius' name from the list of the heretics, on the ground that he had been negligent in not testing Sergius' doctrine, but nothing more.

The artists of Rome, always politically equal to any situation, had anticipated Leo's pronouncement. In the middle of the century, they gave Honorius I a place beside Saint Agnes in her memorial church, Santa Agnese fuori le Mura. She is depicted high up in the mosaic of the semi-dome of the apse, a solitary figure set against the golden background of eternity. From the left, Pope Symmachus approaches her reverently; and on her right stands the controversial figure of Honorius, holding a model of the church which he had founded, perhaps in the hope of thereby purchasing her intercession. Thus, when the Pope in Constantinople declared Honorius a heretic, the artists of Rome had long since accepted him into the glorious host of their saints. Remarkably enough, the picture in which this was done is a masterpiece of Byzantine mosaic art.

The Fourth and last Council of Constantinople, the eighth of the Christian world, held its sessions in the Hagia Sophia, in a setting that for size and impressiveness exceeded any before or since. Only the setting of the Vatican Councils could equal it, they being held in Saint Peter's, Rome. "The inside is too magnificent to appear commonplace, too tasteful to be thought flamboyant. The brilliance and sparkle of

20

sunlight fills it. You could almost say that it was not lit from outside by the sun, but that it generated its own light. So full of light is this holy place." Thus Procopius describes in his book: *De Aedificiis* the "church of divine wisdom." He was an eyewitness and goes on thus in one of the most striking descriptions of the church: "From the round-arch rises a tremendous, spherical cupola of unique beauty. It scarcely seems to rest on its solid substructure, but rather to be a golden bowl hanging free above the interior. Up there in its heights everything merges in the most incredible harmony. One thing depends on another, yet takes support only from what is immediately beneath it. Each detail guides the eye further and so over the whole. Entering the church to pray, your soul is thus conducted on high. You ascend into Heaven. You feel that God is not far away and wish to linger in a place that He Himself has chosen."

Justinian I, Emperor at the time of the Second Council of Constantinople, built Hagia Sophia in the years 532–537. His architects were Anthemios of Tralles and Isidoros of Miletus, who had inherited Antiquity's experience of a thousand years of building. The imagina- *21, 22* tions of these two were creatively stimulated by the wealth of architectural ideas of ancient Greece and Rome and they knew how to adapt these to the needs of the Christian service. The visitor to Hagia Sophia was received by the atrium, in the open space of which twin columns alternated with single pillars in a taut rhythm. Then came the great cross-hall of the marthex, directing his attention at the nine doors that led into God's house. This unfolded before his eye as an intricate, yet simple and extensive space, which is indeed one of the most impressive architectural creations of all time. Roman architects loved circular buildings, the perfection of which one can see in the Pantheon; but the needs of the Christian service required a longitudinal space leading up to the altar, as in the basilica, the market and assembly hall of antiquity. The architects of Hagia Sophia succeeded in marrying the two. Making a square the middle, they covered it with a dome; then to the east and *23* west they placed rectangles to which they gave lower semi-domes that supported the mighty cupola of the central space. The same effect was achieved at the sides by narrow aisles with two-tiered rows of pillars. Forty windows lined the rim of the dome. Two-tiered groups of pillars bounded the sides of the nave and at the same time opened it up. Thus we have a space that is decisively directed at the apse and yet fluid.

Colour and light complete the intention of pillars, walls and vaulting.
24 The colour of the marble in the pillars varies. The walls are lined with slabs of porphyry, dark-green, grey and brown, in vivid pattern. Capitals and round arches are covered with decoration. A reflection of heavenly light comes from the gold-mosaic of the vaulting. In Roman architecture, light illuminates the space, emphasizes divisions and acts as boundaries. In Hagia Sophia, the light conceals joins and softens transitions, with the result that its space goes on and on mysteriously into the boundless.

The Eighth Ecumenical Council met in this glorious building from October 5, 869, to February 28, 870. Again the Council's main concern was the unity of the Church, which was in far less danger from doctrinal differences than from the rivalry between the sees of Rome and Constantinople. Patriarch Photias had ascended the bishop's throne in Constantinople quite illegally, and when the Pope, Nicholas I, refused to recognize him, he summoned a synod and banned the Pope. This first split in the church between East and West shocked all Christendom. The situation, however, was saved by a change in Emperor. In 867, Basil I, the Macedonian, came to power, and the last thing he wanted was a separate church in the East. In agreement with the Pope, Hadrian II, he called an ecumenical council in order to heal or remove the schism. The Council fathers condemned Photias and his supporters, and they fixed the order of precedence of the patriarchs. The Pope in Rome was to come first, followed by the patriarchs of Constantinople, Alexandria, Antioch and Jerusalem in that order. The unity of the church in West and East had been saved once again.

25 The city of Constantinople has many names and faces. The Greeks and Romans called it Byzantium; while to the Christians it has been Constantinople since the day Constantine the Great made it the capital of the Roman Emperors. In 1433 the victorious Turks changed its name to Istanbul. The city straddles two continents. Europe and Asia there meet face to face across the narrow Sea of Marmora, but both share the city's three historical epochs. The image of the city, loveliest from the sea, is still dominated by the Hagia Sophia, now flanked by four minarets, like banners of Islam's victory. The atrium has been destroyed. The mosque has now been turned into a museum.

The unity of the church, saved at the Eighth Ecumenical Council, lasted only until 1054; yet schism, the attacks of the Turks and secularization have not been able to spoil Hagia Sophia.

EPHESUS

IN the middle of the nineteenth century Ajasoluk was just a god-forsaken village. It had a market-place in which an arch or two of a ruined aqueduct stood without point or purpose, and a huge mosque, Isa Bey-Dschami, in which the small congregation of the faithful was completely lost. Then to Ajasoluk came an Englishman. What he was looking for, the villagers could not imagine. He arrived one day from Smyrna and remained. Every day he could be seen roaming about the area between the village and the sea.

This English engineer, M. T. Wood, is one of the earliest figures in the Romance of Archaeology, a story that is far from finished. He suspected that the vanished city of Ephesus lay between the village of Ajasoluk and the sea. Ephesus was where the temple of Artemis, that the ancients had counted among the seven wonders of the world, had been. On the night that Alexander the Great was born, July 21, 356, a man, obsessed with the desire to brand his name in history for all time, set fire to the temple. He succeeded in his endeavour, for the name of Herostratus has been immortalized and is known throughout the world as that of the man who burned down Ephesus. Alexander the Great had the temple rebuilt, and the writings of antiquity are full of descriptions of its magnificence. Wood had read these, and he also knew that the Goths, on one of their early incursions into the Roman empire, had destroyed the temple in 262, after which the Emperor had had it rebuilt once again.

One day the villagers of Ajasoluk learned that the Englishman had gone; but it was not long before he returned with some men and a load of picks and shovels. He then recruited some able-bodied villagers and with his little army of diggers went out to discover the seventh wonder of the world. What he did find, after many laborious trial-digs, proved to be the theatre of a Roman city. However, Wood remained convinced that he had found the site of the lost city of Ephesus. He spent his days out in the countryside, and at night he pored over the ancient books. Seven years he searched and worked in this way, and then chance came to his aid. He found a stone on which was an inscription from the days of the Emperor Trajan giving details of the road the statue of the goddess was to take, when it was brought on the occasion of the great festival of Artemis from the temple to the theatre. Wood followed up this clue and discovered the temple, which, though ruined, was still huge and its sculpture incomparable. It was, of course, where it had always stood, it was only that over the centuries the silt from the river Kaystros, which flows through Ephesus, had pushed out the land by five miles, so that the city was no longer on the sea.

By 1877, when Wood's account of the wonders of Ephesus, which he called *Discoveries at Ephesus*, was published, the temple of Artemis was no longer the show piece of archaeology. One hundred and forty miles north of Ajasoluk, Heinrich Schliemann had found the legendary town of Troy and the world's attention was on that. This was the beginning of the golden age of archaeology in Greece, Mesopotamia and Egypt, and Ephesus seemed to have been almost overlooked.

One cannot help wondering whether Wood and his helpers had only read half the old books that had things to tell about the city, for ancient Ephesus was not just a temple and there was as much more to look for. Long before there had been a temple there, it had been a city. The great poet Homer lived in Ephesus, and he has described the meadows that flank its river, the Kaystros. Heraclitus, one of the first of the Greek philosophers, was one of its sons, and he is supposed to have deposited his writings in the temple of Artemis there. At the time of Christ's birth, Ephesus was one of the great cities of the antique world and its harbour was unsurpassed anywhere in the Mediterranean. The Persian royal highway began at Ephesus, thus giving the city the whole of the known world for its hinterland. It cannot have been easy to say whether it was greater as a centre of trade, or as the home of the goddess Artemis. Pilgrims came to the temple from the whole of the Mediterranean area and beyond. Keepsakes from Ephesus have been found all over the antique world, and because of this the archaeologists of the Austrian Institute told themselves that there must be more to be found there than just a theatre, a temple and a few streets; so, in 1895, they began planned excavations, which indeed are not yet complete.

In 1904, it was decided to investigate the ground along the Arcadiane, the main street of ancient Ephesus. Soon they had uncovered the remains of columns and walls that seemed not quite as old as what had been found hitherto. Gradually the lower masonry of a peculiar large structure came to light. It was in three parts: a court enclosed by colonnades, then a long hall of three naves. In the court was a small round building. They had discovered an early Christian basilica! Outer court, baptismal chapel and church. Such was the obligatory plan. Christian Ephesus had come to light again.

"And the same time there arose no small stir about that way. For a certain man named Demetrius, a silversmith, which made silver shrines for Diana, brought no small gain unto the craftsmen: whom he called together with the workmen of like occupation, and said, 'Sirs, ye know that by this craft we have our wealth. Moreover ye see and hear, that not alone at Ephesus, but also throughout all Asia, this Paul hath persuaded and turned away much people, saying that they be no gods, which are made with hands: so that not only this our craft is in danger to be set at nought; but also that the temple of the great goddess Diana should be despised, and her magnificence should be destroyed, whom all Asia and the world worshippeth.' And when they heard these sayings, they were full of wrath and cried out, saying, 'Great is Diana of the Ephesians'. And the whole city was filled with confusion: and having caught Gaius and Aristarchus, men of Macedonia, Paul's companions in travel, they rushed with one accord to the theatre. And when Paul would have entered in unto these people, the disciples suffered him not. And certain of the chiefs of Asia, which were his friends, sent unto him, desiring him that he would not adventure himself into the theatre. Some therefore cried one thing, and some another: for the assembly was confused; and the more part knew not wherefore they were come together. And they drew Alexander out of the multitude, the Jews putting him forward. And Alexander beckoned with the hand, and would have made his defence unto the people. But when they knew that he was a Jew, all with one voice about the space of two hours cried, Great is Diana of the Ephesians."

The history of the Christians in Ephesus begins here with this account, which is one of the most interesting in the Acts. And is it not all very familiar: the manufacturer not wanting to lose his market, the

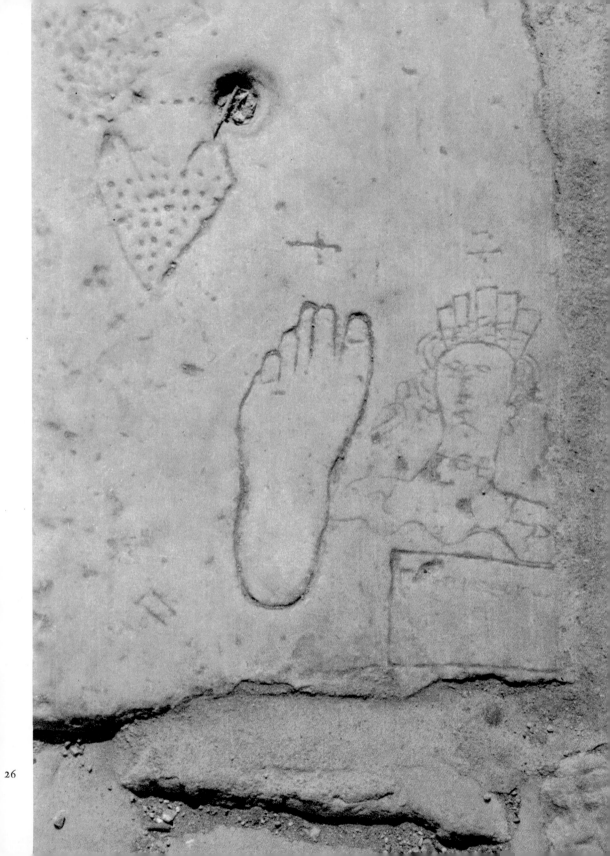

29

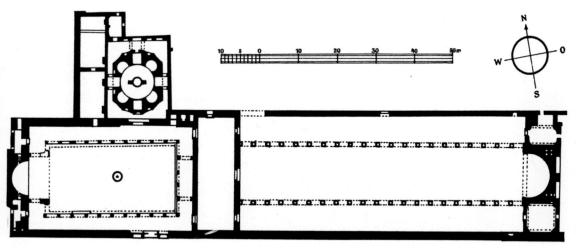

30

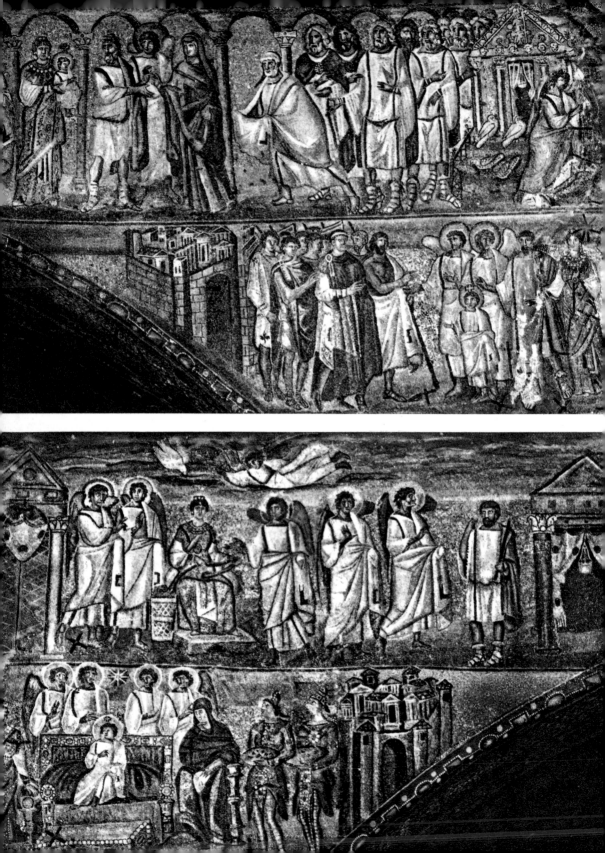

43

crowd raging for hours on end and not knowing why? This was the beginning of Christianity's assault on the ancient gods, which culminated three hundred years later in this same Ephesus, when the Council's great decision changed the face of the world. The observant can still find traces of its activities in the streets of the ruined city. Near the temple, one grateful pilgrim to the temple, apparently cured of some ailment in his foot, has scratched a bust of the miracle-working goddess and the crude outline of his restored limb in the marble paving. Some Christian has corrected him, scratching the victorious symbol of his faith, the cross, above the goddess's head and also on the foot, to show *26* that the cross alone can heal.

The Austrians could not hope to come across a Christian building from the time of the Apostles, but as there was an important Christian community in Ephesus not long after their famous visit, there could conceivably have been an early church. Here, however, they were disappointed. An inscription of two lines was found, which mentioned Archbishop Johannes, who is known as the author of a history of the church that appeared in the Syrian tongue about the year 529, that gave a probable sixth-century date. Christian buildings of the sixth century are not in themselves sensational; that it was of that date appeared to be confirmed by a second inscription discovered on a wall of the outer court. This consisted of more than sixty lines and was a pastoral letter which Bishop Hypatios had had engraved on the wall near the church door, an original idea. Hypatios was known to have been alive in 531. This pastoral, however, was itself sensational, for it told that this was the church in which the Holy Virgin had been proclaimed the Mother of God. This altered everything, for it meant that the Austrians had discovered one of the earliest Christian churches, for this must have been the Church of Mary in which the third general synod, the Council of Ephesus, had met in the year 431.

At the beginning of the fifth century, Christian thought was influenced by two different schools. One was centred in Alexandria, the other in Antioch. The Alexandrians employed metaphorical comparisons in explaining the Bible. Cyril, the Patriarch of Alexandria, explained the nature of Christ by saying that the divine nature of the Lord permeated His human nature as fire does a glowing coal. The theologians of Antioch, on the other hand, were direct and sober in their approach. One of the greatest of them, Nestorius, patriarch of Constantinople, declared that Christ's divine nature dwelt in the man Jesus as in a temple. There was no love lost between Cyril and Nestorius. Alexandria was jealous of Constantinople, the Emperor's new capital. Nestorius' first sermon in Constantinople was devoted to Mary, the Mother of God. He said: "Recently it has come to my ears that again people in our midst are worrying themselves to death over the question: was Mary the Mother of God? Did she give birth to God? Or was she the mother of a man? Indeed, has God a Mother? If so, then one cannot rebuke the heathen, when he speaks of the mothers of his gods. And Paul must be a liar, when he says that Christ's divinity had no father, mother or genealogy." The Church had for a long time been calling the Mother of God, Theotochos, that is: giver of birth to God. Nestorius untiringly sought to stigmatize this concept. Mary was Christotochos, giver of birth to Christ.

Cyril was highly indignant over this. Having secured the backing of Pope Celestine I in Rome, he attacked Nestorius with all the weapons of those early theologians, and they were not fastidious in their choice of them. Nestorius gave as good as he got. The old enmity between the churches of Alexandria and Antioch had found fresh fuel and a new impetus, and the Church itself was threatened by their quarrel and the subsequent confusion. Nestorius exerted himself to the utmost. He succeeded in getting the Emperor to agree to his suggestion that a Council should be held, hoping that the majority of the fathers would condemn Cyril and the Alexandrians. On November 19, 420, Theodosius II invited all metropolitans to come to Ephesus. Thus, Nestorius got his council, but from the start things took a different turn from what he had expected. Theodosius had fixed Whit-Sunday 431 as the day of the opening session, but as the fathers from Antioch and their patriarch, Johannes, had not arrived, the opening was postponed. On June 22, the Alexandrians lost patience and Cyril, as patriarch of Alexandria and representative of Pope Celestine I, opened the Council. The Emperor's representative protested and Nestorius, not wanting to appear before the Council without his supporters, remained in his quarters. The Alexandrians took full advantage of the situation. On the very opening day, the Council rejected the doctrines of Nestorius, deprived him of his office of bishop and expelled him from the priesthood.

The Council met in the Church of Mary in Ephesus, which the *27*
Austrian archaeologists rediscovered in 1904. Its site is still marked by
scattered fragments of pillars and masonry, but it calls for patience and
the ability to imagine and understand, if you are to conjure up a picture
of the building as it was in 431. It is a good example of how the history
of the Church is not just recorded in the writings of its Fathers: buildings and pictures often have even more to tell.

You entered the church from the Arcadiane, first into an outer court *28*
ringed with columns, the atrium. Some of these columns and pillars
have recently been re-erected. In the middle of this atrium a fountain
played. One short side opened in a semicircle forming a mighty apse.
Colonnade, apse and fountain formed an impressive open space. In the
left-hand long wall was a door that led into a circular vaulted space. In
its circular wall was niche after niche, the walls between being decorated *29*
with great crosses. Four steps led down to a marble basin let into the
middle of the floor. This circular room was the baptisterium, the
baptistry.

In the second short wall of the atrium, that facing the rounded apse,
were three doors that led into a short transverse space, the narthex or *30*
vestibule of the church proper. A further three doors led from this into
the church, which had three naves, the central one towering high above
the lower side-aisles, from which it was separated by slender marble
columns. The central nave ended in a semicircular vaulted space, the
apse. On either side of this apse, the side-aisles were enclosed to provide *31*
vestries. The nave was roofed with open beams. The church was 470
feet long, but it was not only its size that made it impressive. One must
imagine it being filled with splendid murals, mosaic and sculptures.
This is suggested by the floor mosaic found in the outer court. This is *32*
like a rare carpet, ornamented with polygons and lattice-design.
Triangles form a giant round shield, and the whole is enclosed by a
lovely border of foliage. The unknown artists have used mostly red, ochre,
black and white for their colours.

Now, walking through the ruins, we must regret the loss of what were
probably great paintings and sculptures. Even so, the surviving masonry *30*
has important things to tell us. The ground plan corresponds to that of
the great basilicas with which the Emperor Constantine the Great
founded Christian architecture, erecting them at the Holy Sepulchre in

Jerusalem and at Christ's birthplace, Bethlehem. He also used it when he built the church of Hagia Irena, the first Hagia Sophia and the Church of the Holy Apostle in his new capital, Constantinople, and again in Rome to which he gave Saint Peter's, Saint Paul Without the Walls and Saint John Lateran. The Church of Mary in Ephesus is just as important as these in plan and setting, but when you compare them you find that there is one difference: none of the others have the mighty round apse in the outer court that the Ephesus church has, and this seems to indicate that it was not built by Constantine. The mystery of this apse was first solved in 1912, when a building from the days of the Roman emperors, 860 feet long and 100 feet wide, was discovered, surrounding the Church of Mary. The apse of the church's atrium had been part of this building, as had the apse of the church proper which still stands, an impressive ruin.

31

At first, the use of this ancient building was not known, but later they came to the conclusion that it must have been either the university or the bourse. The Christians in Ephesus included people of rank and influence, but one must doubt whether they were important enough to be able to use such buildings to help them build their church. Only the Emperor could have taken over one of the most important buildings in the city for such a purpose, and we know that Constantine had been just as generous and lavish, when building other churches. When he wanted to build a Christian church, he had no consideration for the buildings of the past. But the choice of Ephesus as site for such a church must have been deliberate. When one sits among the ruins of the great church and looks across the skeleton of the old city to the distant sea, one wonders what it was caused Constantine to include Ephesus among his favoured cities. Do the ruins hold the answer? On the eastern slopes of the hill called Pana Dag lies the sanctuary of the Seven Sleepers. There, in 1900, a structure with a cupola was found. It was in the middle of a cemetery and had been erected over a catacomb. Individual finds identified this as the cave of the seven holy youths, who had fled from their city during the persecution of Christians under the Emperor Decius and only woke up again when Christianity had been flourishing in their land for centuries. According to the legend this city was Ephesus. On top of the hill, where the Turks later erected a small fort, itself long a ruin, the archaeologists one year later unearthed the church of Saint John, where the evangelist was buried. This is one of the mightiest structures of Byzantine architecture, its dome competing in size and splendour with that of Hagia Sophia in Constantinople. On the second hill, near the village of Ajasoluk, which since 1922 has been called Selçuk, they found a memnaion, one of those small churches that used to be erected in memory of great men of the church. Bishop Gregory of Tours (540–593) recorded that John wrote his Gospel on a hill on the fringe of the city of Ephesus. Was this a memorial erected on that hill? Down below, in the city itself, are the ruins of a church of Saint Luke, traditionally supposed to have stood over the grave of the apostle, whom we have to thank for the account of the disturbance caused by Demetrius.

It is a historical fact that Saint John the Apostle was in Ephesus in the year 66. Did Mary, whom Christ, as he died, entrusted to his favourite disciple, also live there? There are two accounts of the last years of the Virgin Mary: according to one, she never left Jerusalem and died there twelve years after Christ's ascension in the presence of all the Apostles, being buried near the Garden of Gethsemane. The other version has it that John took her with him to Ephesus, where she died. Both accounts say that shortly after her death, she was taken up into heaven.

Both versions still have their adherents. The claims of Ephesus seem to be supported by a letter, which the Council Fathers sent in 431 to the priests and congregation of Constantinople. This says: "By pronouncement of the bishops, Nestorius has been condemned as a heretic in the city in which John the theologian and the Mother of God, the Holy Virgin . . ." the rest of the sentence is missing. The accepted method of completing it is with the word "lived", only the adherents of the Jerusalem version dispute this. The supporters of Ephesus have yet more evidence on their side. In 1891, two French priests in Smyrna read the account of the visions of the Westphalian visionary, Anna Katharine Emmerick, and there found a description of the house in which the Virgin Mary died and of her grave in Ephesus. They set out to look for the house. In the woods on the Ala Dag they found the ruins of a small church. This corresponded to Katharine Emmerick's description. Since time immemorial, local peasants and woodmen have called the place where the church was found, Panaja Kapoulü, the house of the Holy

Virgin. Archaeologists examined the structure and found it to belong to the first half of the fourth century and to be standing on the remains of walls that appeared to have been built in the first half of the first century.

In the fourth century, Ephesus was one of the holy places of Christianity, and the Emperor Constantine had every reason to present it with one of his great basilicas. That he dedicated it to the Virgin Mary could have been respect for tradition, and so could Theodosius II's choice of Ephesus for the Council. What more fitting place could there be in which to decide the dispute between Nestorius and Cyril over Mary's status? This was not finished with the pronouncement of the first session, of which Nestorius said: "Who was judge? Cyril. Who was accuser? Cyril. Who was bishop of Rome? Cyril. Cyril was everything." When, on June 26 and 27, the bishops of the Antioch school finally appeared, a counter-council was set up which, in its turn, banished Patriarch Cyril from the church. This led to a sort of open warfare. As on the night when Herostratus set fire to the temple, or on souvenir-maker Demetrius' great day, a sort of frenzy took possession of the city.

Could Aurelius Augustinus have prevented it, if he had been there? He was the greatest theologian among the fathers invited to the Council, but he never attended it, for he died even before the Emperor's invitation reached his seat at Hippo in North Africa, then being besieged by *33* Vandals. The oldest picture we have of him is in a mural from the library of the Lateran Palace in Rome, which is eleventh-century work. In those days a portrait was not meant to record the mortal features of the subject, so much as his soul and office. These were the more important, and here the unknown artist seems to have succeeded significantly. Augustine is sitting in a wide chair, a large white garment covering his slender body. His thin neck carries an energetic-looking head. This is how a Roman senator turned Christian could have looked. The great book lying open in front of him is an indication of his other calling. You can believe that this is Augustine, the Father of the Church, whom we now revere as the Church's greatest theologian.

No authentic portraits of Nestorius or Cyril have survived, but we have one of Theodosius II, the man who finally decided the outcome of the Council. It is a contemporary bust, now in the Louvre, and it does *34* not make him very impressive. He has a narrow head that tells of long generations grown weary in the exercise of power. There is a sceptical expression round the mouth, and the eyes are pensive. The face is dominated by the big nose of the southerner, but there is not enough forehead to balance it. The line of hair comes down almost to his eyebrows, so that instead of a high forehead doing so, it is left to a diadem to indicate the possession of power. Had the art of portraiture become debilitated? Or was Theodosius II a sceptical philosopher on a throne?

Theodosius was an adherent of Nestorius right up to the first few months of the Council, then, in the autumn of 431, he turned against him, expressed a wish never to hear his name again and banished him to Upper Egypt, the very confines of the Empire. Thus, on October 30, Cyril entered Alexandria in triumph, the theological and political victor, and it seemed that the cry raised by the Council Fathers on July 10 and 11 had been heard: "God save Celestine, the new Peter! God save Cyril, the new Paul. One Celestine! One Cyril! One faith for the synod. One faith for the whole world!" The true victor was Pope Celestine II, who, prior to the Council, had told Cyril to "cut out this festering sore (Nestorius) by which not just one member, but the whole body of the Church is being corrupted."

The picture one has of the Council of Ephesus is not a pleasant one. To many it was just an exhibition of bickering and pigheadedness. However, great events cannot be judged solely by the human, sometimes all too human forms they have taken. In the last resort, the one who triumphed at Ephesus was not Cyril, but Mary, the Mother of God. The people of Ephesus grasped the implications better than many later critics did. Hearing the pronouncement of the first session, the people flocked to the Church of Mary, cheered the Council Fathers and conducted them in torchlight procession to their quarters. When you read of that, you understand why Nestorius took a whole company of imperial troops with him to Ephesus. He knew what the people thought of him and his doctrine. This torchlight procession is itself significant in another way, far more important than the mere triumph of Cyril. The days, when the people of Ephesus used to carry their goddess Artemis in torchlight procession from the temple to the theatre were then not so very far away. The famous statues were probably still standing. One of them was found during the excavations of 1956. There is a majestic look about the goddess's face. A garland of fruits

35

31

serves as her necklace, and below it are three rows of breasts, like ripe fruit. The slender column of her lower part is decorated with heads of lions and stags, which also constitute the glory round her head. In her, the virgin mother of the gods, the goddess of hunting and the ancient goddess of fertility had become one.

On that memorable evening, many of the citizens of Ephesus, who as boys had paid homage to the goddess, cried: "The Holy Virgin is Mother of God! Down with Nestorius!" The fight for Ephesus that Paul had begun, was over. No one any longer called out: "Great is Diana of the Ephesians." It was not Nestorius, but the great goddess, Artemis, virgin and mother in one person, who had lost the day. Her place was now taken by the Virgin Mary, the Mother of God, and in building her church, the foundations and masonry of a pagan school were taken and incorporated into the Christian structure. They heightened the available structure and adapted it, in the same sort of way as at the Council of Ephesus the image of Artemis, virgin mother-goddess, was adapted, being merged into and superseded by that of the Holy Virgin Mary.

Painters are usually most ready to immortalize the great events of history. Has no brush been used to depict this great occasion? How ungrateful artists must be, if that were the case, for in the Mother of God the Council gave them one of their greatest subjects. Rightly, the victress of Ephesus has had a triumphal arch put up to her, but this is not to be found among the ruins of that city that stand near the Turkish *36–39* village of Selçuk, but in the Basilica of Santa Maria Maggiore in Rome. Pope Sixtus III (432–440), the successor of Celestine I, commissioned it to glorify the life of Mary. Remarkably, it was not the official version of the Gospels that was followed: it was to the so-called pseudo-Matthew gospel and the Arabic account of Christ's childhood that the artists and their spiritual advisers went. Thus a Roman triumphal arch and oriental imagery combined to glorify Mary, the Mother of God. The walls on each side of this arch are divided into four picture areas. The pictorial story begins in the top left-hand corner with Mary receiving the annunciation from the Archangel Gabriel. To the right of this an angel is instructing Joseph not to abandon Mary. The story is interrupted by the top of the arch, on which is placed the throne of divine wisdom that represents the Apocalypse, and on its steps are

45

54

PP. III
SPECU BEATI BENEDICTI REGLARE VITA SERVANTIBUS
VIRTUTU NULLU MAGIS EST MEDULLATU QUA QD OFFERTUR ALTISSIMO DE
CARITATIS. HOC IGIT ATTENDENTES. CU OLI CAUSA DEVOTIONIS ACCESSISSEM AD LOCU
VRE QUE BEATUS BENEDICT SUE CONVERSIONIS PRIMORDIO CONSECRAVIT
INSTITUTIONE IPIUS LAUDABILITER DNO FAMULANTES. NE PRO
SPIRITUALIS OBSERVANTIE DISCIPLINA TORPERET. APOSTOLICU VOBIS SUBSIDIU
IMPENDENDU. SPERANTES QD IDE BEATISSIM BENEDICT NRE DEVOTIONIS
ET PRECIB APUD PIISSIMU PATRE ET IUSTISSIMU IUDICE COMMDABIT
NECESSITATIB PUIDERE. SEX LIBRAS USUALIS MONETE VOBIS ET SUCCESSORIB
CAMERA BEATI PETRI SINGULIS ANNIS PCIPIENDAS CONCESSIM. DONEC
VOBIS ESSENT UTILITER ASSIGNATE. STATUENTES UT EA QUE
SUEVISTIS PCIPERE DE MONASTERIO SUBLACEN. VOBIS ET SUCCESSORIB
MINIME NEGARENTUR. POSTMODU AUTE CU REVERSI FUISSEM
VRIS AD NRAM PRESENTIA DESTINASTIS HUMILITER IMPLORANTES
IPSA INALIQUO CERTO LOCO DIGNAREMUR PPETUO STABILIRE.
SEX LIBRAS PCIPERE VALERETIS. NOS IGITUR HABITO
ASSENSU. IA DICTAS SEX LIBRAS VOBIS ET SUCCESSORIB VRIS PCIPIENDAS
ANNIS DE ANNUO CENSU CASTRI PORTIANI CONCEDIM. ET CONCESSIONE
PRIVILEGIO CONFIRMAM. NULLI ERGO OMNINO HOMINU LICEAT HANC PAGINA
CONCESSIONIS ET CONSTITUTIONIS INFRINGERE VEL EI AUSU
IRE. SI QUIS AUTE HOC ATTEPTARE PRESUPSERIT. INDIGNATIONE OMNIPOT
ET BEATORU PETRI ET PAULI APOSTOLORU EIUS SE NOVERIT

Peter and Paul. Underneath them is a scroll with the inscription "XYSTUS EPISCOPUS PLEBI DEI" (Bishop Sixtus to God's people), so that the donor, Pope Sixtus III, has got his name in the most prominent position. The picture-story then continues towards the right with the presentation of Christ in the temple. In the strip beneath this there is, starting from the left, the three kings worshipping, and, on the opposite side, an unusual episode from the pseudo-gospel of Matthew, describing how the idols fell from their plinths as the Jesus' parents were escaping into Egypt with their child. This brought the King of Sotine hurrying up in order to punish them, but he was converted. Beneath this again we see Herod questioning the Three Kings about the purpose of their journey, while, across on the left-hand side, the infant children of Bethlehem are being murdered on Herod's orders. On the sides of the arch the space for pictures becomes narrower and narrower and finally there is room for only representative pictures of Jerusalem and Bethlehem, which are identified by inscriptions. The lambs of the Apocalypse crowd their gateways, presumably representing Christians hurrying to the holy places.

There is nothing new in these picture-stories, for these were familiar events in early Christian art; it is only that here they have been retold and reinterpreted. In the picture of the Annunciation, Mary is sitting on a throne like a princess of the Byzantine imperial house, with her palace shown on her left. Winged angels stand round her as ladies-in-waiting and guards. The messenger of the Annunciation is made to appear quite secondary as he floats in the blue sky above them, together with the dove of the Holy Ghost. The presentation in the Temple is represented as a procession of the Byzantine imperial court: the Mother of God, the child Jesus on her arm, appears from the left out of the pillared hall of the palace, with a suite of angels and court-officials. Joseph seems less God's foster-father than an imperial master of ceremonies. His subordinate position is obvious from his clothes. He only has a short cloak worn across his shoulders, while the angels, as bodyguards of the Mother of God, are all in the long *pallim*. The most regal and splendid garment is reserved for Mary, who is holding her child out in both hands. A halo surrounds the child's head, above which a cross hovers. This solemn procession is being met by the Prophetess Hannah, a noble Roman matron. Old Simeon comes hurrying up from

D

33

the right to receive the divine child. Behind him, you see a throng of prophetic, divinely-inspired old men. The whole of the Old Covenant with its prophets and priests are pouring out of the Temple in order to see the Word made flesh and the promise of the Old Testament fulfilled.

These mosaics elevate Mary, the unknown girl from Nazareth, insignificant village in Palestine, to the imperial family. The princess is here made the Mother of God. This tremendous event has been portrayed by artists who were among the greatest masters of their day. They knew how to depict groups of excited people and make them talk with gesture of hand and head and with looks. The drama is told in the glowing colours of mosaic. In no other work of the age are the stones so daringly and beautifully put together. The pictures are composed of patches of colour such as you get in modern paintings. The graduations are fine and exact. These masters did not have one white, but many. They could depict the correct intensity of light of the time of day with light grey, light blue or violet. Here, in this triumphal arch of Santa Maria Maggiore, the imagery of the East, the life at the imperial court at Byzantium and all the colour that a thousand years of Greco-Roman art had collected have been combined in a many-voiced chorus of praise to Mary, the Mother of God. Never before or since has a Council's resolution been given such a memorial.

CHALCEDON

"RELIGIOUS questions came before all other matters. For, if God the Almighty is gracious to us, it is our duty to maintain and improve the condition of our realm. Now that doubt as to the true faith seems to have arisen, as the letter of the blessed archbishop of Rome, Leo, demonstrates, we have decided to convene a Sacred Council in Nicaea in Bithynia, in order that the truth may be tested in agreement with everyone, so that in future there can be no more doubt or disagreement in this respect. Therefore, Your Holiness and as many wise and orthodox-minded bishops subordinated to you as you please, shall be in Nicaea on the coming September 1st. Unless the military situation prevents it, we ourselves shall personally attend this venerable synod."

Thus the circular letter in which Emperor Marcian invited the metropolitans of the Empire to a Council in Nicaea for the purpose of revising the resolution passed at the so-called Second Council of Ephesus, the Robber Council, and dealing with the doctrine of the one nature of Christ. When the Council Fathers were all assembled in Nicaea, the Emperor transferred the Council to Chalcedon, this being close enough to the capital for him to be able to deal personally with business in Constantinople and at the Council. The Council of Chalcedon is regarded as one of the most important gatherings of the Church in history. More than six hundred bishops are said to have attended it. Many of its sessions were presided over by the Emperor Marcian and his wife, Pulcheria. Father of the Council and its directing spirit was the Pope, Leo I, whom history has rightly dubbed "the Great". We are better informed about this Council than about any others in antiquity, for the official minutes of the proceedings, the lists of attending bishops and a considerable correspondence have been preserved, yet by some trick of Fate, no trace of this important council can be found in the place where it met and held its sessions. Today, Chalcedon

35

is called Kadiköy. Looking across the Bosporus from the beach there, you will see across the Bay of Kadiköy the silhouette of Istanbul. Kadiköy is a small port with a modern appearance that might place it anywhere in the world. In 1824, Helmut von Moltke noticed an eminence rising gently some 300 yards in from the shore. Then, it had no buildings on it. Today it is all built over and called the Field of Windmills. Walking its streets, you will not see the least trace of the church of Saint Euphemia, which stood outside the town here on the road to Nicomedia and in which the Council met. There are no ruins even on which one's imagination could work, so that all one has to go by is the description given by Euagrius, a lawyer from Antioch, who continued Saint Eusebius' history of the church up to the year 594. In writing of this Council of Chalcedon, he says:

"So, they assembled in the basilica of the martyred Euphemia, which stands near Chalcedon in the land of Bithynia, no farther than two stages from the Bosporus, at a pleasant, gently rising place, so that those going to the sanctuary of the martyr have no difficulty in getting there, but suddenly find themselves on top and in the midst of the compass of this house of God. Looking out from there, as from a watchtower, you overlook it all. The sanctuary lies opposite Constantinople, and consists of three big oversize rooms: one is an open longitudinal court with pillars all round it; the next is almost the same as the first in length, breadth and pillars, but it has a wooden roof; towards the East there is an adjoining domed room ringed with the most beautifully worked columns, all of the same material and height. These pillars support a gallery under the roof, so that from there you can both honour the saint or take part in the Litany, just as you please. Within the domed space, facing East, there is a lovely bounded area, in which is the coffin wherein the holy relics of the Saint lay. The coffin is of silver very artfully wrought."

Euagrius' description, too, seems very intelligent. From it, it is obvious that Saint Euphemia's was one of the great churches of early Christian architecture in which space for the congregation was combined with memorial church. Atrium, basilica and church follow in that order, a pattern that Constantine the Great set in his church on Mount Calvary in Jerusalem and which was also followed in, among others, the church of Santa Lorenzo before the Walls in Rome, which also has the gallery Euagrius describes in the original room enclosing the martyr's grave.

The church of Saint Euphemia has disappeared without trace, but we have pictures of some of the men and women who attended the Council there. In the museum of the castle of the Sforza in Milan there is a marble head of an Empress of the sixth century, some ten inches high. Her waved hair is like a garland round her forehead and the back of her head. A diadem of pearls and a cap keep it in place. The nose has been broken, but even so the face retains its nervous, alert expression. *41* Big eyes look out at the world expectantly, and the mouth is small and firm, lips closed. The Empress seems to be actively looking and at the same time listening to some inner voice. She is Pulcheria, grand-daughter of Theodosius I and wife of Marcian, whose influence on the government was apparent even during the rule of her brother, Theo-dosius II. In fact, when Cyril, patriarch of Alexandria, wished to put the point of view he represented at the Council of Ephesus before the imperial house, he wrote not only to Theodosius II, but also to the latter's elder sister and "teacher". This letter leaves one in no doubt whom Cyril considered to have the better understanding of the matter.

On July 28, 450, Theodosius had a fall from his horse and died, and the crown passed to Pulcheria, who was then already fifty—and un-married. Pulcheria was clever and, realizing that alone she could not deal effectively with either the intrigues of the Court or the Huns, who had invaded the realm under Attila, she married General Marcianus, who, on August 24, 450, was crowned emperor at her side. Flavius Marcianus was not of princely family. He was one of the soldier-emperors. He was born in Thrace in the year 396, son of a Roman officer, and chose to follow his father's profession. Later historians made him out a sort of Byzantine old sweat who cut a comical figure beside the gifted Princess Pulcheria, but contemporary sculptors saw him very differently. There is a large bronze figure in front of the church of San Sepolcro in Barletta, Apulia. It is sixteen feet high and has stood there *42* for 1,500 years, but not undamaged. The top of the head above the diadem is missing and the legs have been renewed. This great figure is wearing two tunics, a breast-plate and a sash. The diadem of pearls and precious stones shows it to be the statue of an emperor, for that is what they all wore from the days of Constantine the Great on. The raised right hand now grasps a cross, though earlier it would have held a sceptre. In the left hand is a stone ball representing the earth, instead of the ancient globe.

The centuries may have damaged the statue of Marcian and in their way supplemented it; but they have not been able to harm his posture or expression. The statue is not just great and commanding in dimensions. The armour and clothing have been accurately and carefully modelled, and they emphasize the man's physical strength. In all probability the original was carved in the studios of the Court in Byzantium, where, in the sixth century, they had gone back to the sculptural traditions of the ancient Greeks. How good that was can be *43* seen from the Emperor's head: he looks you full and square in the face, and there is none of that anxious expression of the eyes and rigidity of feature that make the statues of the end of the fifth century look so frightened. It is a very human face, but that does not prevent it having the dignity and remoteness of a ruler of the world. Mouth, nose and eyes have the calm strength of the soldier. The deep lines between nose and mouth tell that he has known setbacks and defeats, and in the eyes there is that same flexibility of intelligence that dominates the Empress Pulcheria's face. Her small marble image and this great bronze head are akin not only in hair-style and diadem. The statue and, so to speak, official portrait of a Roman Emperor, depicts a man who was worthy of the crown and crown-princess of Byzantium.

"Unless prevented by the military situation, we ourselves shall personally attend this venerable synod," wrote Marcian in his letter of convocation. Though Attila and his Huns were almost at the door, the military situation did not altogether prevent him from taking part in the Council of Chalcedon; but the situation being what it was, and Pulcheria having more experience of such matters, Marcian was content to leave questions of faith to his wife, who thus became one of the main figures of the Council. She thought that the influence that the patriarch of Alexandria had exerted in Byzantium ever since the days of Cyril was altogether too great, and she wanted means of offsetting it. She found what she needed in the then Pope in Rome, Leo I.

"The dignity of Peter is not lost, if one who is unworthy falls heir to it," he wrote. This pronouncement which was to be of great importance for the papacy in the future, applied as little to him as to anyone. He was a worthy successor to Peter, pious and eager to keep the faith pure, a teacher and statesman in one. Leo did not himself go to Chalcedon, but sent five legates who ran the Council. At the first session, held on October 8, 451, in the church of Saint Euphemia, Dioscurus, head of the Robber Council of Ephesus, had to appear to answer the charges laid against him, and on October 13 he was deposed and expelled from the Church. The minutes of the session end with these words: "Christ has deposed Dioscurus, the murderer! A just judgment, a just synod, a just Council."

October 10 was a more glorious day, for on it the Council devoted itself to its main task of determining the true faith. The discussion centred round the dogmatic letter that Leo I had written in 449 for the synod of Ephesus and which Dioscurus had at the time suppressed. This is one of the great historical documents of the Church, the fineness of its style competing with the clarity of its thought. Reading it today, you can understand why at the end of its being read out to them, the Council Fathers exclaimed: "That is the faith of our Fathers, the Apostles. Everybody believes that. Peter has spoken through Leo! That is what the Apostles taught. Pious and true is Leo's teaching. That is what Cyril taught. Eternal memory to Cyril! Leo and Cyril have taught the same. Anathema to those who teach differently."

Leo's dogmatic letter was summarized in the declaration of faith proclaimed at the sixteenth session, over which the imperial couple presided. This says: "So, following the holy Fathers, we all unanimously preach one and the same Son, Our Lord Jesus Christ, perfect as deity, perfect as human being, true God and true man consisting of sensible mind and body, identical with the Father in divinity and identical with us in humanity, similar to us in everything, except sin; for all time created by the Father the Godhead, but finally for our sake and the sake of our salvation born of the Virgin Mary, the Mother of God, in accordance with his humanity." To counter the Monophysites it was declared that the divinity and humanity of Christ were two natures, unmixed and not transformed, in one person; and to counter the Nestorians, that these two natures were together in that person, not separate and not divided.

No pope before Leo had so insisted on the precedence of the Roman see before all the others. At its last session, the Council of Chalcedon

39

resolved that the Bishop of new Rome, meaning Constantinople, had the same rights as the Bishop of old Rome; but that the patriarch of Constantinople occupied second place in the church, coming after the "Archbishop of Rome", and this, despite his friendship with Marcian and Pulcheria, Leo refused to recognize. Many historians have reproached him for this, on the ground that in this lay the origin of the future schism that was to separate the Byzantine church from Rome.

Though Leo I was a determined opponent of the claims of Byzantium, the oldest picture that we have of him is a Byzantine painting. It is to be found in one of the most important places of world history, the Forum in Rome, where an old Roman building was early converted into the Church of Santa Maria Antiqua, and this the Popes of the eighth century seem to have liked best of all Rome's churches, for they were continually commissioning artists to paint and repaint its walls. Today, it is just a ruin among ruins, and none of the murals that Pope Paul I (757–767) gave it have survived, except some bits in the left aisle. There you see Christ enthroned in the midst of a long line of male saints, all painted full face and figure and with names to identify them. On the left of Christ's throne are the Church Fathers of the West, on the right those of the East, among whom figures Gregory of Nazianzus. Leo I appears among the Church Fathers of Rome. The ravages of time have almost obliterated his face; but it is narrow and disciplined, surrounded by a glory. One eye still looks at you, the other has gone. The Pope's slight figure is dressed in the vestment of a priest and in one hand it holds a large book, symbol of his being a Father of the Church. To the right of his halo is written in Greek: Leo Hagios, Saint Leo. In those days, the art of new Rome flourished in Rome, and as this did not aim at giving true likenesses, we find that all these saints are looking back at us from the next world with expressions of supernatural strictness. They hover in white robes in the blue of the wall which represents heaven. The individual lines up with the rest, filled with sacred duties as one of the company of Our Lord, raised above all personal emotions and cares.

What was it the Council Fathers cried at Chalcedon? "Peter has spoken through Leo! That is what the Apostles taught! That is what Cyril taught! Leo and Cyril have taught the same!"

They lauded Leo and yet made him just one among the rest in the

HIC SVPERIS DIGNVS REQVIESCIT PAPA BENIGNVS
LÆTVS DE FLISCO SEPVLTVS TEMPORE PRISCO
VIR SACER ET RECTVS SANCTO VELAMINE TECTVS
VT IAM COLLAPSO MVNDO TEMERARIA PASSO
SANCTA MINISTRARI VRBS POSSET QVOQ RECTIFICARI
CONCILIVM FECIT VETERAQ IVRA REFECIT
HÆRESIS ILLISA TVNC EXTITIT ATQ RECISA
MOENIA DIREXIT RITE SIBI CREDITA REXIT
STRAVIT INIMICVM CHRISTI COLVBRVM FEDERICVM
IANVA DENATO GAVDET SIC GLORIFICATO
LAVDIBVS IMMENSIS VRBS TV QVOQ PARTHENOPENSIS
PVLCRA DECORE SATIS DEDIT HIC SIBI PLVRIMA GRATIS
HOC TITVLAVIT ITA VMBERTVS METROPOLITA

INNOCENTIO IIII PONT MAX
DE OMNI CHRISTIANA REP OPTIME MERITO

QVI NATALI S IO BAPTISTÆ ANN M CC XLIII PONTIFEX RENVTIATVS
DIE APOSTOLORVM PRINCIPI SACRA CORONATVS

QVVM PVRPVREO PRIMVS PILEO CARDD EXORNASSET, NEAPOLIM A
CORRADO EVERSAM S P RESTITVENDAM CVRASSET INNVMERISQ
ALIIS PRECLARE ET PROPE DIVINE GESTIS PONTIFICATVM SVVM
QVAM MAXIME ILLVSTREM REDDIDISSET

ANN M CC LIIII BEATÆ LVCIÆ VIRGINIS LVCE, HAC LVCE CESSIT

ANNIBAL DE CAPVA ARCHIEP NEAP
IN SANCTISS VIRI MEMORIAM ABOLETVM VETVSTATE EPIGRAMMA R

60

61

BONAVENTVRA

OPTAVI ET DAT ET SEN SUS ET VOCAVI TVERIT IN ME SPS SAPIE ET PPOSVI ILLA RE GNIS ET SEDIBVS

SIOHES EVAGLISTA

SANTHEVS EVG

66

67

procession of the divines that have passed through Church history since the days of the Apostles. The Byzantine painters of Santa Maria Antiqua in Rome did the same thing three hundred years later.

THE LATERAN IN ROME

EIGHT ecumenical synods of the church were held during the 544 years that elapsed between the first Council of Nicaea and the fourth Council of Constantinople. Then followed 253 years without one Council being held, and, when the Church did go back to the old tradition and summon its Ninth Council, both the purpose of the Council and its place of meeting had changed. The eight previous Councils had been convened by the Roman and Byzantine Emperors, and they had all met in the East. The first few Councils of high Middle Ages were Pope's Councils and they met in the papal residence, in the palace and basilica of Saint John Lateran. In the eastern Councils it was the question of Christ that had been the central one; the western Councils, on the other hand, were concerned first and foremost with the internal and external life of the Church.

45   Alessandro Galilei completed the balcony side of the basilica of Saint John Lateran about the year 1735. There is a vast framework of colossal half-pillars and half-columns, between which are five doors and as many loggias, dark caves that make one think of the colonnades of the Coliseum. They seem to be waking to a delayed after-life in order to give the basilica the dignified appearance due to its status as "Mother and head of all the churches of the city and of the globe." This, too, would seem to be the purpose of the host of the saints whose huge statues surmount it with baroque pathos.

46   The way inside is by one of the oldest doorways in the world, for these are the ancient bronze doors of the Curia, the assembly building of the Roman Senate. You come into a five-aisled pillared basilica. The side-aisles are vaulted and the central nave has a richly carved and gilded ceiling, while against its pillars stand enormous thirteen-foot-high marble statues of the Apostles, telling witnesses to faith to accompany one's progress to the altar.

This is where the five Lateran Councils met, only in those days the church itself looked different. There are three remarkable murals in the left side aisle of the church of San Martino ai Monti in Rome. The centre one is that of the ratification of the Council of Nicaea, which we *47* already know. To the right of it is a picture of the interior of the old Saint Peter's, and to the left, the inside of Saint John Lateran as it looked before Pope Innocent X had Pamphily reconstruct it. This is the church that Constantine the Great built in 313 on the foundations of the Lateran Palace, a five-aisled pillared basilica with a transept and apse. The mural in San Martino ai Monti shows, on the left, its slender marble pillars with their Corinthian and Ionian capitals. The roof-frame is open over the high central nave. Innocent told his architect Borromini that he was to do the church in the contemporary form, but retain as much of the Constantinian structure as possible. Comparing the mural in San Martino ai Monti with a photograph of the baroque *46, 47* structure shows that not only have the proportions been retained, but that the new structure gives the same impression of space. In the transept, on the other hand, the apse seems to have been altered. Pope Leo XIII had it replaced by a new choir between 1876 and 1884. The triumphal arch that Constantine set up on tall Corinthian pillars still leads into the transept, where there is still the altar canopy that Giovanni di Stefano put up in 1367, shaped like a Gothic steeple. If you can imagine the altar in the mural as not being there, you will have the setting in which the first four Lateran Councils met.

The reconstruction of the seventeenth century not only destroyed the *48* appearance of the interior, but also rendered a number of monuments, sculptures and other things homeless. They were given refuge in the cross-aisle, a real masterpiece by Vasalletti, who was a Roman and a real artist in marble, and which he finished about the year 1230. The covered walk surrounding the court has small double-pillars. Some are plain, some are fluted; they twist like ropes of two strands. Coloured mosaic gives extra life to the marble. The shapes of animals emerge out of the luxuriant foliage on the capitals and portals. Stepping from the baroque basilica into this medieval place of meditation and prayer, you could believe you were looking at the meeting-place of the First Lateran Council as it really was. But it is not. The cross-aisle was completed twenty-five years after the Fourth Lateran Council was held, and, like the papal altar in the transept, the first Lateran Council it served was the Fifth of 1512–1517.

In 1122, Guido Count of Burgundy, then Pope Callistus II, and the Emperor, Henry V, signed the Treaty of Worms, thus ending the investiture dispute over the question whether or not the Emperor had the right to bestow ring and crosier upon the imperial bishops. Callistus II wished to cement this new peace in the church by holding a general council, and this met from March 18 to April 6, 1123, in the Lateran. The ceremonial sessions were held in Constantine's basilica, as depicted in the Santa Martino ai Monti mural, and an aula was used for working sessions. This was pulled down in 1586, when Sixtus V built the new palace. The Council reaffirmed previous regulations, gave a fresh impetus to spiritual care, devoting its attention to simony, the truce of God, and the protection of crusaders and pilgrims to Rome. New regulations were laid down for ordinations and church offices; and the sacraments figured prominently in the discussions. There are few
49 written records of the transactions of the Council or documents dealing with those taking part in it, and the pictorial arts serve us little better. We have no idea what the Pope looked like, though we have his bishop's throne. It is in the cloister of Saint John Lateran. A podium and two marble pillar-steeples provide it with a splendid frame. These latter are akin to the pillars of the cross-aisle and, like them, were made in the fourteenth century. The half-dilapidated marble seat is supposed to have been the bishop's chair of Saint Silvester, the Pope of the time of
50 Emperor Constantine. Even now there is a solemnity in its marble, and the plants on its sides are still firm and clear-cut.

In the cathedral in Constance, where the sixteenth Council met between 1414 and 1418, there is an empty sarcophagus, on top of which lies the life-size effigy in stone of a bishop wearing his mitre and with his crosier beside him. The pontifical robe, beautifully folded, rests lightly on the body, and the priest's garment follows its curves, pliant and melodious. The oblong, bearded face is full of quiet harmony. This is fifteenth-century work, and you can see from it how the heyday of German sculpture of the age of chivalry is over. The monument honours the most important personage of the First Lateran Council, Bishop Conrad of Constance, who was canonized by Pope Callistus II on March 28, 1123. It was no mean man who was thus paid the honour of being canonized at an ecumenical Council. Conrad was a member of the ducal house of the Guelphs. As Bishop of Constance (934–976) he not only built three churches in the city where he had his see, but also made three pilgrimages to the Holy Tomb in Jerusalem. The archdiocese of Freiburg, which formed part of the see of Constance, revered him as its patron.

When Pope Honorius II died in 1130, sixteen cardinals elected Gregorius Papareschi, Pope. He was a friend of the powerful Roman family of the Frangipani. As Pope, he assumed the name of Innocent II. The other cardinals, feeling that they had been taken unawares, elected their own pope, Peter Pier Leoni, and he took the name of Anacletus II. Innocent inhabited the Pope's proper residence, the Lateran, and the anti-pope Anacletus, barricaded himself in the Vatican. His death there on January 25, 1138, ended the schism. Innocent II decided to seal the restored unity of the church with a Second Lateran Council, which began on April 4, 1139. The bishops and cardinals who had supported Anacletus, "the Pope from the Ghetto," were deposed. Usury was forbidden. Jousting was frowned upon, and from that time on monks were no longer allowed to study law and medicine. Marriages contracted by secular priests and monks were declared invalid. Of greater historical impact was the decision to transfer the choice of bishop to the chapter; and there was an ominous side to the accusation of heresy brought against Arnold of Brescia, the canon. In fact, this latter plunged Rome into domestic confusion that lasted forty-four years.

The Papareschi, a member of whose house Innocent II was, were all-powerful in the district of Trastevere. Innocent restored its most important church, Santa Maria, making it one of the stoutest and loveliest Roman basilicas of the thirteenth century. In its apse, Christ is crowning his mother, Mary, while the patrons and builders of the church, which was founded in early Christian days, watch the ceremony. Their ranks are brought up by Pope Innocent II, who comes walking swiftly from an imaginary room towards the group, bringing them the church of Santa Maria in Trastevere, a model of which he has in his hands. His face, which is turned full towards us, has obvious individual features and is the only one really alive. You will see people like him in the narrow streets of Trastevere today, where the real Romans still defy the levelling forces of the new metropolis. This mosaic ranks high in the history of Roman art. It is the work of Byzantine masters, who had previously been working in Venice. It gave a new lease of life to Roman pictorial art, that had been in the doldrums since the eleventh century.

There is a most unusual thirteenth-century reliquary in the monastery church of Kappenberg in Westphalia. It is one of those head-reliquaries, where the relic is contained in a man's head on a stand. This head has been cast in bronze and gilded. It does not portray Christ or any of the saints, but the Emperor Frederick I Barbarossa, and has been deliberately made as a portrait, for it not only depicts the Emperor's features, as one sees when you compare it with other portraits of him, but also gives the essence of his character as we know it from written sources. In the severe modelling of the cheek bones and the ceremonial hair-style, the traditional attributes of the ruler mix with the accepted idea of the chivalrous, noble, fascinating emperor. It is the same with the eyes, which originally were made of big precious stones. This gave the portrait something of the awesomeness which goes well with those old pictures of majesty and its bearers, something of the mystery that both intimidates and attracts. This effect is heightened by the stand, which has dragon's feet and four angels with turrets between them carrying the head. The stand thus represents the heavenly Jerusalem, which is mirrored on earth in the Empire, the crown of which Frederick wore. This reliquary is evidence of a remarkable process, for here personal likeness and impersonal attributes of sovereignty are merged. This is the first German portrait head we know, and it is of the Emperor of the time of the Third Lateran Council.

In 1159, Orlando Bandinelli of Siena was elected Pope and took the name of Alexander II. He was an old enemy of the Emperor's and so Frederick Barbarossa set up an anti-pope against him. This began a struggle between Emperor and Pope which was to prove a bloody one. Anti-popes came and went. Barbarossa destroyed Milan, which had risen against him, but then he himself suffered a crushing defeat at the hands of the Lombardy Union at Legnano. In 1177, Emperor and Pope made peace in Venice, and Alexander III sealed this with a Third Lateran Council that lasted from March 5 to 22, 1179. These anti-popes had always been a danger for the church, so it was now decided that in future a two-thirds majority should be necessary before any pope could be elected; that anyone wanting to be a bishop must be at least thirty years of age; and anyone supplying weapons or armour to the Saracens should be excommunicated. The Cathari, a sect that had come into being in Southern France, were condemned.

What pictorial records there are of the Council have nothing to tell of these things. They are solely concerned with Alexander III's triumph at Venice on, which the Council set the seal. The Venetians wanted to immortalize that great event in a series of frescoes, which Pisanello painted in the Doges' Palace, but they have been destroyed. The people of Siena were more fortunate: there, in the *balia* room of the Palazzo Pubblico, you can still see the sixteen murals in which *54* Aretino Spinello recorded the history of Alexander III. In his painting Spinello tried to preserve the naïve massive style of Giotto, which, of course, here suited his subject. In these murals legend has taken precedence over historial fact. In one of them, you see Alexander II, the great son of the city of Siena, entering Rome, riding a white horse. His severe-looking head is crowned with a tiara and his right hand is raised to bless. His mount is being led by two men, who are none other than the Emperor Frederick Barbarossa and the Doge of Venice, Ziani. On the right, the walls of the Eternal City await his arrival: to the left, behind the cavalcade, a stylized landscape slopes up and away to the horizon, falling on one side to the sea and a harbour, where the ships that brought the Pope from Venice ride at anchor.

The Lateran in Rome has been the scene of many historical events, but few have been more important than those of the three autumn days of 1215. On November 11, 20 and 30, a Council held session for the fourth time in the basilica and palace of the Lateran. The Middle Ages were approaching their classic peak. Chivalry and scholastic divinity were in the process of perfecting the magnificent medieval system of life and thought. Cathedrals towered up, and beauty, which is a glint of truth, filled the world. The emergence of new classes and orders lent dynamism to a time of peace. The townspeople were striving for power and the mendicant friars got a hearing. Emperor and Pope were worthy of the time. On the throne of Saint Peter sat Innocent III and on that of Charlemagne, Frederick II.

In a private house in Lanuvio in the Alban hills is an art collection which, since the nineteenth century, has included an enormous marble *53* head, depicting a person of obvious importance. Some of the features are reminiscent of the Emperor Augustus, others again of Constantine the Great. In 1948 an archaeologist, Guido von Kaschnitz, examined it and found it to be fourteenth-century work and not made in antiquity. It is the head not of Augustus nor Constantine, but of the Emperor Frederick II of Hohenstaufen. Frederick is regarded as the first modern statesman on the throne; many indeed regard him as the enlightener of the Middle Ages. What seemed so modern to later generations, must have given the thirteenth century its richness, and this the Hohenstaufens made resound all over the world. Frederick traced his office back to Augustus and Constantine; and Byzantium and Rome are indeed united in this head of him; though the mouth and eyes are those of the long generations of the statues set up on the cathedrals of the West, whose Emperor he was.

On July 25, 1215, Frederick II was crowned King of Germany for the second time; and in November of that year the Fourth Lateran Council confirmed him Emperor of the Holy Roman Empire. Never before had a Council solemnly confirmed the choice of an emperor, and it has never been done since. The explanation for this unusual step is to be found in the relations between Emperor and Pope. Henry IV had died young, in 1197, when Frederick was three years old. The Empress Constance got Pope Innocent III to act as his guardian, but he could not prevent the Guelph, Otto IV, being made king in Germany. When Otto, however, set about preparing to attack Sicily, his ward's hereditary land, Innocent laid him under a ban. The German princess deserted Otto and, in 1211, decided that Frederick should be the future emperor. The Fourth Lateran Council sealed this victory of Frederick over his opponent. Innocent III was long regarded as a king-maker and was accused of using the Curia to achieve a world dominion; yet the picture of him, that the Benedictines revere in their church of Subiaco, depicts a very different kind of person. He occupies a niche and is wearing the vestments and tiara of the Pope. In front of him he holds a large placard, which he is handing to the Benedictines with a flourish of his other hand. On the placard is the text of a bull issued by him to the order.

Does this face tell us anything about Count Lothario di Segri, the accomplished jurist and theologian, who became pope at the age of

70

75

GREGORIVS XII
PONT. MAX.
ANTEA
ANGELVS.
CORRARO

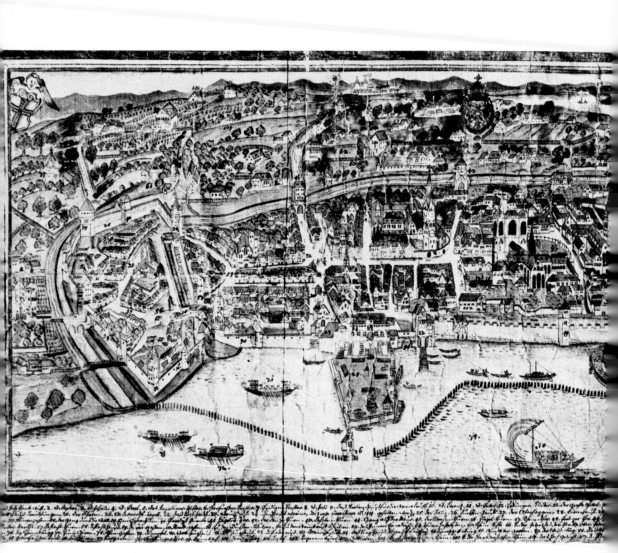

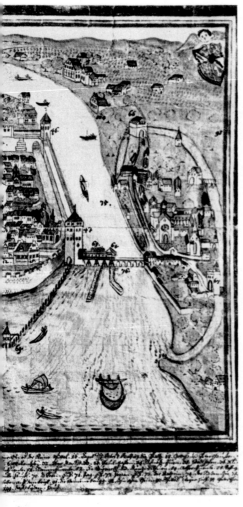

80

81

Sizung der Kirchen-
latin im Münster.

Papst Iohannes schenkt dem Koenig Sigismund eine
geweihte goldene Rose.

thirty-seven? Here the same thing has been done with the marble head of Innocent's imperial ward: the artist who painted it at the beginning of the fourteenth century, went back to pictures in the catacombs in Rome and borrowed general features from Byzantine icons to obtain a general impression of a pious, venerable holder of an office, into which he then worked the personal features of Count di Segri. The result is a portrait that corresponds to what we know of the Pope of the Fourth Lateran Council. "As did the Fathers of old," he invited the bishops of West and East, the abbots of the orders, the chapters and the Christian kings, to come to Rome. He wished to confirm Frederick II as emperor, but his main concern was spiritual welfare. Most of the seventy resolutions passed by the Council are still among the Church's statutes. They condemned not only the heresies of the Cathari and Waldensians, but made annual confession and the taking of communion at Easter obligatory; they also laid it down that no diocese might be without a bishop for longer than three months, and enjoined bishops to see that sermons were preached in the vernacular. Finally, the Council resolved on a new Crusade that was to leave Sicily on June 1, 1217. This was not just the resolve of "the Pope as absolute Lord of the Whole Church", but the resolution of a majority of those attending the Council, who were many. We know of 404 bishops, and there are said to have been 800 abbots. The Emperor and the kings had all sent representatives, so that Christendom was really united once again and well represented.

This Fourth Lateran Council was well abreast of the times. Courageously and realistically it decided on reforms that are still effective. The Fifth and last Lateran Council, however, tried to turn back the clock of world history. It tragically failed the needs of its day. It met in 1512, when the world was a very different place, and was followed by the two Lyons Councils and that held in Vienne. At the great reform Councils of Constance and Basle, the Popes had had to fight against the conciliar theory, but both Council and Pope also endeavoured to carry through such reforms as the Church needed in that new age. The reason for calling the Fifth Lateran Council was the fact that King Louis XII of France had convened a rival council in Pisa, as part of his feud with Pope Julius II. It was in order to disarm this that the Pope summoned the Eighteenth General Council to meet in the Lateran. It

E
49

was opened on May 10, 1512. The fifteen cardinals and seventy-nine bishops attending it were almost all from Italy. The Pope had no real difficulty in checkmating the rival council, and it lost all its significance, when he himself died on February 21, 1513, and was succeeded by Leo X.

It was easy enough to convene a Council for no specific purpose, but it was not so easy to get the Council fathers to go home again once they had assembled. They were not content to get the rival council dissolved, but asked for reforms that affected the head of the Church as well as its members. In his opening sermon, the general of the Augustines, Giles of Viterbo, was emphatic that: "Man must be transformed by the holy, not the holy by man." The Spanish memorandum to the Council openly demanded: "The Court must start with the house of the Lord." The Pope of the last Lateran Council was Leo X, Giovanni Medici, second son of Lorenzo the Magnificent. Raphael made him the subject of one of the loveliest groups in the history of art, which now hangs in the Palazzo Pitti in Florence. Raphael, the young genius from Urbino, lent magic to his day, in that he glorified its humanistic longings in paint. He gave to his people and landscapes a harmony of gaiety, wisdom and beauty, that you seldom find in real life. Leo X had pursued the Ideal on a study-journey in Germany, the Low Countries and France; he had sought it in the writings of the Humanists and in the paintings of the Renaissance. He strove for it in a household that acted up to his motto: "Let us enjoy being Pope, since God has made us one."

This Medici prince was naturally ugly, and Raphael made no attempt to beautify him. He portrays the Pope engaged in his humanistic pursuits. In front of him lies a Neapolitan Bible, that later found its way to the Berlin Kupferstichkabinett. Leo has been reading it and looking at its miniatures, and still holds a magnifying glass in a rather elegant hand, which he is casually resting on the table-cloth. His face is fleshy, its expression surly, and there is a suspicious look in the eyes that are glancing sideways at his cousin, Cardinal Giulio de Medici, who later became Pope as Clement VII. He appears just to have walked in, thereby disturbing the Pope in his intellectual pursuits, and is telling him something that obviously does not please His Holiness, though it seems to be affording a certain malicious pleasure to Cardinal Ludovico de Rossi, who is standing behind the Pope's chair, looking slyly out from the picture. Raphael has observed the three with cool objectivity, and, in this his last great commissioned portrait, he has again tried out all the possibilities of colour. This group is accounted one of his master-pieces. It is immersed in red, but who will count the different nuances of red that here are brought into unique harmony?

Leo liked red, the colour of pleasure, victory and heroes. Not that Leo was a hero. The combination of intellectual and physical prowess that characterized the great men of the Basle Council was quite foreign to him, the epicure and aesthetic of the late Renaissance. The cry that judgment must begin with the House of the Lord must have sounded boorishly discordant to his delicate ear, and he must have heaved a sigh of relief on March 16, 1517, when he was able to close the Fifth Lateran Council and once more devote himself to his hedonistic tastes.

The voices of those calling for reform in the Church were then unable to reach him. The adherents of the conciliar theory no longer had a platform on which to expound their ideas. In October of that same year, 1517, Martin Luther came forward with his 95 theses. Thus reform, for which members of the Church had struggled and which the last Lateran Council had so shamefully neglected, began in a quite unexpected quarter. Was Leo X, who was Pope until 1521, aware of this? At all events, he does not seem to have understood its causes and world-wide consequences.

LYONS

LYONS is a well-known name, but not a well-known town. The tourist by-passes it in his haste to get to the Riviera. Only the merchant knows it as the centre of the silk industry and for its great Fair that is held every year in March. To those on a fleeting visit it seems just another industrial centre, the same as so many others that have shot up here and there, a place without true face or heart; but if you stay a bit longer and explore the sea of houses between Rhône and Saône, you will discover that this is not the case. On the right bank of the Saône there is an old quarter, the haunt of artists, a place of taverns and tom-cats. It is called Saint Jean after the cathedral that dominates it, its choir facing the bank of the Saône, and its late Gothic façade rising from a quiet, not too big close. Going in, you are surprised at the size of the twelfth- and thirteenth-century interior.

If you know the history of the places you visit, you will understand them, their peoples and buildings, better than those who do not; but often such knowledge can be a burden and so it is in Lyons. "Oh, day of wrath, day of calamity and lamentation," cried Thaddeus of Suessa, Frederick II's Sicilian judge of the supreme court, on July 17, 1245, when addressing Pope Innocent IV as he sat on the bishop's throne in the severe choir of the cathedral here, which then, as now, must have been flooded with coloured light from its tall slender windows. Then, it was the scene of one of the greatest tragedies of European history, the meeting place of the First Council of Lyons.

"Out from the sea comes a beast, full of the names of slander and abuse. It has the paws of a bear, the roaring throat of a lion and its other limbs are those of a panther. It opens its jaws to blaspheme and similarly bombards the House of the Lord and the Saints who dwell in heaven. It tries to crumble everything with its claws and iron teeth and to trample everything with its feet. Observe carefully the head, body and rear of this beast, Frederick, the so-called Emperor, and if you find abomination and crime there, then protect your unsullied hearts from its wiles with the shield of truth!"

Thus Pope Gregory IX of Emperor Frederick II. Again and again, for two hundred years this feud between Emperor and Pope had shaken the West, but in the struggle between Gregory IX and Frederick II it acquired apocalyptic proportions. Gregory put the Emperor under a ban and unleashed propaganda against him in which no holds were barred. Frederick gave as good as he got. In one of his manifestoes it says: "And we assert that he is himself that monster, of which it is written: 'And there went out another horse that was red: and power was given to him that sat thereon to take peace from the earth, and that they should kill one another. . . .' "

Gregory's death on August 22, 1241, looked as though it would end this dreadful quarrel, especially when to succeed Celestine IV, who died before he could be inaugurated, the Cardinals chose Sinibald Fieschi, Count of Lavagna, who took the title of Innocent IV. He was regarded as being friendly to Frederick, and the Emperor opened negotiations with him to try and end the squabble over the rights of Emperor and Church in Italy, which was the heart of the dispute with Gregory. The two arranged to meet at the Emperor's residence of Narni in Umbria, but in the night of June 28, 1244, the Pope suddenly left Sutri on horseback with a small suite and rode to the port of Civitavecchia, where he boarded a ship and sailed to Genoa.

Whether this journey was the result of the Pope's suddenly taking fright, or whether he had never really intended to negotiate with the Emperor, it is impossible to say; but the Pope's next steps appear to have been in accordance with a plan laid in advance. He went to Lyons, which was still within the Empire, but a Free City and devoted to its archbishop, who was the Emperor's enemy. Lyons stood at the intersection of the long-distance routes between the Rhine and the Mediterranean, between France and the Alpine passes, and Innocent could have chosen no better place from which to fight the Emperor.

On January 3, 1245, Innocent sent out invitations to a general council to meet in Lyons. Bishops came from France, Spain and England, but few from the rest of the Empire, for Frederick had forbidden them to attend and blocked the roads. As a result, the Thirteenth General Council was not well attended. It was estimated that at the most 140 to

150 bishops were there. It was inaugurated by the Pope on June 28, 1245, the eve of the Feast of Peter and Paul, in the cathedral of Saint John in Lyons. Innocent IV told the Council fathers that he was plagued by five torments: the sins of the priests, the loss of the Holy City, the dangerous situation in the Empire of Constantinople, the Mongol attacks on Europe, and, last and not least, the persecution of Church and Pope by the Emperor Frederick II.

The cathedral of Lyons stands on one of the oldest church sites in Gaul. In 1935, masonry and a mosaic floor going back to the days of the Roman Empire were excavated under the choir. On top of this was more masonry, then the present structure of the cathedral, which was begun in the thirteenth century and took four centuries to finish. The choir was built by about 1200. Transept and nave are thirteenth-century work, and in the fourteenth century some of the vaulting and the windows of the central nave were renewed. And at the end of the fourteenth and in the fifteenth century the archbishops decided to

57 complete the building and gave it its late Gothic façade. We do not know whether the transept and nave were already built by 1245, when the Council met. Judging by their structure and form they could have been built in the first half of the thirteenth century. The nave has the

58 usual triple form. Rows of columns in the shape of bundles of slender pillars and half-pillars separate the high central nave from the lower side-aisles. Steep pointed arches rise from the columns, above them low triforia break the flat surface of the wall. In a higher, third storey, are windows, thrusting up into the vaulting with its stiff framework of ribs. This is the classical structure of the Gothic cathedral, yet you cannot help noticing that its effect is different from that of the cathedrals of Amiens or Paris. Its stone has remained heavy and corporeal. The difference between the south and the north of France is evident even in their buildings. This different relationship is even more evident in the choir; the pedestal wall is ornamented with lovely blind-arcading with shallow pillar-bases and round-arch friezes. In the half-pillars, the fluting is made deeper. In the triforium, these groomed pilasters find their way free from the emprisonment of the masonry and become free pillars. The round of the apse and these grooved pilasters and pillars are a heritage from the architecture of ancient Rome. In 43 B.C. Lyons was a Roman colony and later became a flourishing town with import-

ant buildings. Goethe said of artists that "the earth recreates them, as it has given them being from the beginning"; that also goes for art-forms.

The bishop's throne in the centre of the apse wall also has this *59* ancient Roman simplicity and size. This is the position it used to occupy in the basilica of the early Christians. Three curved steps lead up to it; the two sides and flat bench between them are of marble. The sides also act as arm-rests though they do not look conducive to ease. There is no sort of decoration. Who occupied the bishop's throne had other things than his rest to think about; the dignity of his office was more of an embellishment than any decoration or picture.

Pope Innocent IV would not have found this a hard seat, when, from it, he formulated his accusation of Frederick on June 28, 1245. Although he mentions the Emperor last of the five plagues that he said were afflicting him, he started his campaign against him on the very opening day, pronouncing him a heretic, accusing him of associating with unbelievers and of breach of treaty and sworn word. His chief complaint, however, was that the Emperor had captured a Genoese fleet carrying more than a hundred prelates to the Council summoned by Gregory IX for Easter Day, 1241, in the Lateran in Rome. Frederick was defended by the best lawyer at his court, Thaddeus of Suessa, a Sicilian. His defence was pertinent and well-weighed, but Innocent was not having any of it and tore his argument to shreds. On the second day, Thaddeus of Suessa did manage to obtain an adjournment in order to get fresh instructions, but it did him no good: judgment had already been passed. At the session of July 17, 1245, Frederick II was found guilty of perjury, of disturbing the peace and of heresy, and the Council deposed him as German king and as Emperor of the Holy Roman Empire of the German Nation. "Oh, day of wrath, day of calamity and lamentation," cried Thaddeus, but the triumphant Pope did not understand him.

Innocent IV died in the "wrath" of which Suessa had complained in Lyons. As he was involved in the struggle of extermination he was waging in southern Italy with the sons and grandsons of Frederick, whom he had cursed at Lyons, death overtook him on December 7, 1254 at Naples and he was buried in the cathedral there and over his grave they erected one of those great, gable-crowned tombs of the late

thirteenth century. What remained of it 331 years later was re-erected
by the Archbishop of Naples. On the sarcophagus is a recumbent statue
of the pope and above it are two inscriptions. The upper one says:
"Here rests in God worthy, kind and joyous Pope de Fiesco, buried
here of old, a holy, just man, protected by the banner of Heaven, so
that, when the world was collapsing with fear, he might occupy the
Holy City. In order to restore order, he convened a Council. He
restored the ancient Law. Mightily did he defeat heresies. He set up
again the walls that had fallen and defined the Faith. He overthrew
that enemy of Christ, the Snake Frederick." In this inscription Hannibal
of Capua has recorded the opinion of Innocent IV held by the people
of his day. Some unknown artist has carved this as part of a relief which
was executed in 1585. In this the Madonna is seated in the middle and
on her left Pope Innocent kneels, his tiara modestly placed on the
ground beside him, while the Infant Jesus leans towards him.

The sixteenth century had no great faith in the portraiture of the
Middle Ages, and the archbishop of Naples and his sculptor obviously
have not taken the stone figure of the Pope on the sarcophagus as a
serious portrait. Today, however, we know that it is a good characteriza-
tion of the man. He lies there in full pontificals, head on a cushion,
wearing the papal double crown that was customary up to the time of
his successor, Clement V. His face is a triumph of the art of portraiture,
that is the presentation of the whole person. Here is an old man who is
not only ugly, but repulsive. His mouth is pinched, his nose watchfully
alert; the eyes speak of mistrust and greed. Hannibal of Capua's eulogy
does not fit this face, as does the present judgment of history, which is
summarized thus in the *Lexicon of the Popes*: "Innocent, whom Saint
Louis accused of continually exceeding his competence, was important
as a man of law, double-faced as a Pope and devoid of any inner greatness: as a politician ruthless in his choice of means, deposing kings
pointlessly and putting the Emperor, Sancho II of Portugal and Jacob I
of Aragon under his ban. Greed for money, fraudulent cunning and
boundless nepotism made him a hated figure."

Hannibal of Capua's inscription records that it takes the place of a
previous inscription that had been lost. Originally, the cenotaph had
been placed on a high plinth and was covered with a canopy supported
by pointed arches. Innocent IV's tomb is one of the more important

86

88

89

Belehnung des Burggrafen
Friedrich von Nürnberg mit
der Markgrafschaft Bran-
denburg.

och die burgtzwatk, alt zu
remberg Und do praüentn
all praümen und pfiffetend
all pfifer und menglich,
rait hiam

Diß figur stät hie
nach gemält

94

97

98

99

monumental tombs, in which Italian art excelled at the end of the thirteenth and in the fourteenth centuries. Their structure and quality can best be studied in the papal tombs in the church of San Francesco in Viterbo. There in the heads of Clement IV and Hadrian V you see the same impelling honesty: the sculptor has refused to be chivalrous and beautify someone because he had been great, and has shown even the repulsive side of his physique and character.

Frederick II died in Fiorentino, four years before his enemy Innocent IV, on December 13, 1250. Swept away "by envious death", as the chronicler puts it, he died of an illness of the intestines, while his feud with the Pope was at its height. He is not portrayed on his sarcophagus, which is in the cathedral of Palermo, next to that of Henry VI, his father, and that of Roger II of Sicily, his grandfather, and although Giorgio Vasari (1511–1574), the Italian "father of the history of art", stated that Frederick's son, Manfred, king of Sicily, commissioned a German artist to make a monument to his father, this has been lost, unless by it is meant the porphyry coffin which contains his dust. The question of what this great member of the Hohenstaufens really looked like was revived when Guido von Kaschnitz, the archaeologist, discovered the giant marble head of the Emperor, which we have already mentioned in connection with the Fourth Lateran Council. It was *53* Professor Brandi of Bari who thought of searching for unsuspected pictures of the last Hohenstaufen in Apulia, Frederick's favourite countryside, and his search there was rewarded. In the Museum of Barletta, he discovered a thirteenth-century bust of which no one thought anything in particular. What drew his attention to it was its artistic quality; then to his surprise he discovered a damaged inscription that pronounced it the head of Frederick II. *61*

Does this head at last answer the question what this man, who "in strange and wondrous way troubled the world", wanted and what he was? Was he Antichrist, the hammer that smashed the globe, the first enlightener, the first modern statesman? What we see is an old man, whom the storms of life have bent. This is evident in the very inclination of head that leaves no doubt that this is a head that has taken many a blow. Gregory IX excommunicated him, because the crusade he had promised did not come off. Henry VI's talented son was indignant and died under the ban. Innocent IV, on whom the Emperor had been pinning his hopes, had him pronounced deposed at the First Council of Lyons and cursed his family. Petrus of Vinea, one of his most trusted men, defrauded him of very considerable sums, and then in May 1249 his favourite son, Enzio, king of Sardinia, was taken prisoner by the Bolognese. These blows bowed, but did not break the Emperor.

The head wears a narrow diadem to show that it is a crowned head and symbolizing the burden of an Empire that stretched from the frontiers of Denmark to Sicily. The face is most expressive in profile, as it is reproduced here. Looking at it full face, you see its intellectual strength. This is Frederick the thinker, educated in philosophy and natural science, the citizen of the world, friend of Jews and Saracens, a man as familiar with the culture of the East as with that of the West, who surrounded himself with writers and himself wrote treatises on horse breeding and falconry. The open mouth, the eyes and the line of the cheek have an expression of restrained intellectuality, but as a whole it is a bold, masterful head. This is the man who could be as terrible as a Roman emperor, the organizer of the first bureaucracy of the West in Sicily, which he based on the old Roman state.

The unknown author of this head is one of those great sculptors whose portraits of saints and princes are in the cathedrals of Naumberg, Bamberg and Münster. He has both reproduced the physical features of his subject and seen within him and portrayed in stone what he discovered there. He has portrayed more than there is space to mention here, but especially clemency, and has given us the sum of all that had happened to this man and all his qualities. This head makes one feel that towards the end of his life Frederick was plunged in melancholy, and here he seems to be repeating what his predecessor on the heathen imperial throne of Rome, Septimius Severus, said, when he looked back on his life: *"Omnia fui et nihil expedit"*—I have been everything and it has been of no avail.

This man, imprisoned in the diadem of power, was everything, only not the Antichrist and not the beast of the Apocalypse. If from the viewpoint of this empty bishop's throne in Lyons one tries to look back to the heart of the historical events of the Council, all that one sees is the struggle for temporal power in the West. Innocent IV claimed this for the Pope, while Frederick held it rightly to belong to the Emperor. The Pope was a man who knew no moderation and paid no regard to human limitations. He could not see that the chair of Saint Peter was not able to bear this double burden, and that, without a strong temporal opposite pole, the papacy would fall into a vacuum. In order to be able to go on existing Innocent IV's successors went the French way that he had blazed. In the "Babylonian captivity" of Avignon (1309–1377) they were in the power of the French kings, territorial lords whose growing power Innocent had feared as much as Frederick's. Instead of triumphing, the papacy passed through the most dangerous decades of its history. The calamity that Thaddeus of Suessa bewailed on that "day of wrath" in Lyons fell not only upon the sons and grandsons of Frederick, but upon the whole of Christianity.

Is the cathedral the only record of this tragedy in Lyons? The Huguenots and the mobs of the 1789 revolution plundered the cathedral and its treasures and Lyons now has none of the church vessels that the *62* Council used, and no picture or other record of that historic summer. There is, however, another building that served the Pope and the Council, the Manecanterie. Its history is as mysterious as its name, which is said to come from the Latin *mane cantare*, singing in the early morning. In the sixteenth century the building actually was used by the choristers; but in the twelfth century it was a dining-hall for the staff of the chapter; but we do not know the purpose for which it was built. It is to the south, on the portal side of the cathedral, its long wall looking grim and uncommunicative beside the great portal. Pillars, small columns and round arches give it an air of antiquity. Our tidy minds, that have to place everything in a definite time and place, like to date it as eighth-century work. The art historian, however, says that it was built in the last decades of the eleventh century.

*   *   *

In August 1271, Viterbo witnessed a remarkable spectacle. Rainero Gati, the burgomaster, marched at the head of the burghers and *63* artisans to the bishop's palace, near the cathedral. This is still one of the best examples of thirteenth-century architecture. It was built in 1257–1266, and the loggia and steps were added a year later. The palace shows all the defensive elegance of the thirteenth century. The ground floor is tall and high and is carried on big round-arches, above which the side wall is pierced by round-arched square windows. The structure is topped with battlements. A wide, free-standing flight of steps, with something of ancient Roman temple steps about them, leads up to it. Only the front wall of the loggia has survived. The inside of the palace is dominated by the big session hall, an enormous room without pillars covered by a roof with open rafters. The people of Viterbo were proud of their bishop's palace, in which popes had stayed and lived, but on this August day they had other things to think of. Rainero Gatti ordered the carpenters and tilers to remove the roof from the great session hall.

What had happened was this: Pope Clement IV had died in Viterbo on November 29, 1268. The cardinals had all hurried there to elect his successor, but three years later they were still not agreed. It then occurred to the people of Viterbo that it might hurry things up, if their deliberations were to be held in less comfortable surroundings. The idea of removing the roof is said to have originated with the general of the Franciscan order, Johann Fidanza, called Bonaventura. On the floor of the great hall you can still see marks left by the huts that the wretched cardinals had built for themselves after the roof had gone. But by September 1, the Church had a new Pope! The new Pope, elected in such unusual circumstances, was neither a cardinal nor even present in Viterbo. The news of his election reached the archdeacon of Lüttich, Tebaldo Visconti of Piacenza, in the fortress of Acre in Palestine. Visconti, who assumed the name of Gregory X, accepted this call with considerable reluctance; in fact he left his heart in the Holy Land.

This Gregory X was the Pope of the Second Council of Lyons, the fourteenth general assembly of the Church, which he opened on May 7, 1274, in the cathedral there. Many who listened to him had also been there on June 28, 1245, and Innocent IV's indictment speech may still have rung in their ears. But how changed the scene was! The speech from the bishop's throne was that of a noble priest intent on peace and reconciliation. The Council was attended by representatives of all Christendom, including the Emperor Michael of Constantinople. Germany, scarcely represented at the First Council, sent six archbishops and twenty-eight bishops. While Innocent IV had debated measures of defence against the Mongols, Gregory X invited the great Khan to attend the Council. Innocent IV deposed the Emperor. Gregory X was determined to end the long interregnum, the "terrible time without an Emperor" (1254–1274), if need be against the will of the Electors.

Opening the council, the Pope gave the assembly three tasks: to give increased help to Jerusalem, which was in danger; union with the Greek Christians; and reforms in the church. Among the cardinal bishops sitting to the right of the Pope in the choir of Lyons cathedral, was Johann Fidanza, Bonaventura, whose idea had hastened the election of the new Pope in Viterbo. There is a picture of him in the Nicolas Chapel in the Vatican, which is the work of Giovanni da Fiescole, a Dominican brother whose sublime paintings earned him the name of Fra Angelico, the angelic brother. In 1450, he was commissioned to paint the small room in the Vatican palace that had originally been Pope Nicolas V's study. Bonaventura is standing in front of one of those pillar-like walls with which Fra Angelico divided up his great murals of the legends of Saint Stephen and Saint Laurence. He is wearing the simple garment of the Franciscans, the order of which he was the general and the reviver. At his feet, cut across by the edge of the picture, lies the cardinal's hat that was his as Cardinal Bishop of Albano. He is holding a book, the traditional symbol of Fathers of the Church. Bonaventura infused the doctrine of the church fathers and the philosophy of Saint Augustine with the mystical love of Saint Francis. He saw the road of the church as one that led to the wisdom and peace offered by the all-embracing cognition of Christ. His bearded face reflects this peace, and Fra Angelico has also given him that saintly serenity that he so liked to give his portraits. Behind the gracious gentleness, you can see the physical strength and clear intelligence that were just as characteristic of this general of the Franciscans and angelic Father of the Church, Doctor Seraphicus. *64*

The Second Council of Lyons was an assembly of the great men of the thirteenth century, and also a council of the great dead, for Gregory X died on his way back from it, when he was in Arezzo. In the cathedral there, they gave him one of those tombs where the sarcophagus has a Gothic arched canopy. An inscription from 1807 records it as being the work of Margaritone d'Arezzo (1216–1290), painter, sculptor and architect. He, too, is wearing the tiara in death. His large face, its eyes closed, mirror the virtues of which documentary sources tell us. Cardinal Bonaventura died during the actual Council, and on the way from it *68* death also overtook the greatest of its Fathers, Thomas Aquinas. He died on March 17, 1274, in the hospice of the Cistercian monastery of Fossanova, to the south of Rome. In 1365, the prior of the Dominican monastery of Santa Maria Novella in Florence commissioned Andra di Bonainto, known as Andrea da Firenze, to paint the glories of the Dominican Order for the monastery. In what is now known as the Spanish Chapel, he painted one of the great didactic picture cycles of the fourteenth century. The painting on the left wall is dominated by *65* Thomas, talented son of the Count of Aquino, friend of the Hohenstaufens. He is seated on a covered throne, dressed in the black and white garments of the order, holding in front of him the symbolic book of Church teaching, as if it were a precious reliquary. The artist presents Thomas as the most important teacher of Church doctrine and philosopher of the late Middle Ages, whom the Church took into its company of saints as Doctor Comunis and Doctor Angelicus. The face is filled with that great repose for which he was famous, and which was based on unity of belief and knowledge, recognition of God and thought. He took the teaching of the great Greek philosopher Aristotle and introduced it into the spirit of the West, thus constructing one of the greatest edifices of thought in the world.

Although Andrea da Firenze was concerned to paint a programme picture of Church teaching, he has given the round, firm face of his central figure its personal features. According to the old documents, Thomas was tall and upright. He strode through the cloisters of the monastery head up, even when deep in thought. His complexion was that of a grain of wheat. He had a big forehead and a face that was both strong and sensitive. His friends used to say that the fire never went out of it. We have no difficulty in recognizing Thomas Aquinas in Andrea da Firenze's portrait of a Dominican monk.

The fate of Saint Augustine, who died before he could attend his Council at Ephesus, overtook Thomas Aquinas. His teacher and friend, Count Albert von Bollstädt, however, was at Lyons among the Council fathers. He, too, was a Dominican. Thomas had sat under him at Paris and then had gone with him to Cologne in order to found a college for his order there. Albert, who was later called Albertus Magnus, Albert the Great, was a bishop, a diplomat and preacher of crusades. There seem to have been no limits to what he could achieve.

In spite of being exceptionally active in the affairs of this world, he found time to write a philosophical and scientific work that, in its modern presentation, occupies forty volumes. In his day it was a comprehensive encyclopaedia of knowledge. Albert was bishop of Regensburg from 1260–1262. We still have his seal of office, which is formed like an almond-shaped halo and has an inscription round its rim. In the *66* centre is Albert on his throne, mitre on his head, crosier and book in his hands. For a long time this seal went disregarded and to the historian it was just one of many symbols of office and scarcely a life-like picture; but the face that looks at us from Albert's seal has not been given the conventional episcopal dignity. It has a bashed-in nose and a broad mouth. The eyes are deep set. It is an ugly face and we know from documentary sources that the Count of Bollstädt, though a man of intellectual gifts, was far from handsome. The unknown seal-maker has striven after a likeness, and that he has achieved one is confirmed by Tommaso Barisini of Modena who, in 1351, painted the walls of the chapter hall of San Niccolo in Treviso with forty portraits of the saints *69* of the Dominican Order. Tommaso was from Emilia in Modena, and his stolid mentality was fully equal to the task. He painted realistic character studies. Albertus Magnus is sitting in his study, wearing the white cassock and black cloak of the Dominicans. The mitre seems foreign to his lively face. It is obvious that Albert is not concerned with thoughts of his office, but with some idea that has come to him while reading the book lying open on the desk before him. The left hand is hidden and the furrowed face is alive with a sort of piercing perception. There is something uncomfortable about it, and we can understand why this scientific seer was suspected of magic.

At the Second Council of Lyons, Albert's activities were diplomatic. Rudolph of Habsburg had him to thank most of all for the fact that Gregory X recognized him as German king. The "dreadful time without an Emperor" was over. Rudolph's tomb occupies the place *67* of honour in the crypt of the cathedral in Speyer, burial place of many medieval kings and emperors. His life-size statue is framed with an inscription. He is depicted standing on a lion, arrayed in full coronation regalia. The emperor's mantle hangs from his shoulders, the imperial eagle, like an order, on his chest. In his right hand he holds the great imperial sceptre, in his left the orb surmounted with a cross. His long narrow face is further elongated by the crown of the German kings.

When Frederick II died, the imperial throne lost its original significance. "What is to endure in art, must be destroyed in life." The writers and thinkers of the end of the thirteenth century seem to have acted in the spirit of this saying of the young Schiller. The imperial idea was never so praised and honoured as when all its power had gone. Dante Alighieri, author of the *Divine Comedy*, was not the only one romantically to cry for an emperor, who would do what Charlemagne and Frederick II had done. What he expressed in words, painters and sculptors said in their media. Rudolph of Habsburg was never crowned Emperor of the Holy Roman Empire of the German Nation in Rome. He was more a father of his country, fighting to defend it, than Emperor of the West. But, dead, he appeared in all the regalia of the Holy Roman Emperor. Reality, which will not let itself be mocked, corrected this romantic dream, as it were, privately. The world had grown hard and poor. In the plastic arts the so-called rigid style had come into being, and we can see it at its underground work in Rudolph's statue. Beneath the excessive dimensions of the cloak, the body of the Emperor shrinks. Sceptre, orb and crown are too pompous and do not really go with that disillusioned, thin face with its raised eyebrows and deeply furrowed brow. The Count of Habsburg cannot fill the Emperor's robes.

On May 20, 1277, one of the ceilings in the bishop's palace in Viterbo collapsed, killing one of the great figures of the Second Council of Lyons, Peter Rebuli-Giuliani of Lisbon, who, as John XXI had been Pope for not quite a year. The papal historian likes to point out that he was really John XX, because, properly, Pope John XX, who came before Gregory VI, had never been. When Cardinal Roncalli took the name of John XXIII on October 28, 1958, many people were quite disgruntled, for this was tantamount to saying that John XXIII, whom the Council of Constance had deposed, had been lawfully elected. None the less, John XXIII used the name rightly, because if there had never been a John XX then he really was the twenty-third John on the chair of Saint Peter, counting the anti-pope, John XVI.

At the Council of Lyons, Peter Rebuli-Giulani had not yet become involved in the chronology of the popes. He attended as the personal physician of Gregory X. He is portrayed on his simple sarcophagus in

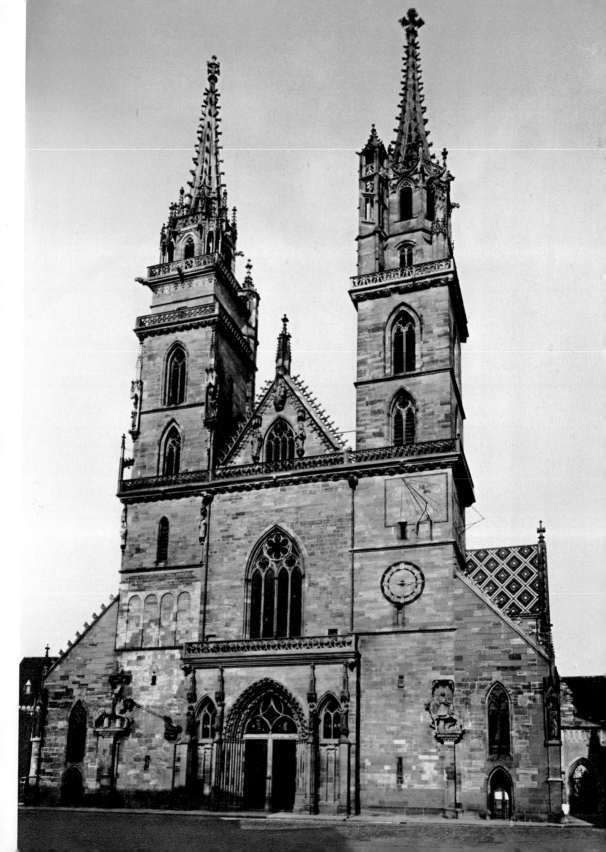

108

110

111

URBS·VENETUM·DEDIT·ORTUM
QUID·ROMA·URBIS·ET·ORBIS
IURA·DET·OPTANTI
CAELICA·REGNA·DEUS

MEMORIAE
EUGENII·IIII
SUMMI·ATQ·OPTIMI·PONTIFICIS
HIC·IN·PACE·GRAVIS·IN·BELLIS·PRO·CHRISTI·ECCLESIA·IMPIGER
IN·INIURIIS·PATIENS·RELIGIOSORUM·AMATOR·AC·IN·ERUDITOS·VIROS·MUNIFICUS
CONCILII·BASILEENSIS·INSOLENTIAM
ADVERSUS·PONTIFICIAM·ROMANAM·POTESTATEM
CONCILIO·FLORENTIAE·CELEBRATO·REFRENAVIT·AC·FREGIT
IN·QUO
IOANNES·PALAEOLOGUS·GRAECIAE·IMPERATOR
ROMANUM·CAPUT·AGNOSCENS
EIUS·PEDIBUS·SE·MULTASQ·EXTERNAS·ET·REMOTAS·NATIONES·HUMILI·SUBSTRAVIT
CONGREGATIO·CANONICOR·S·GEORGII·IN·ALGA·VENET
FUNDATORI·RELIGIOSISSIMO·PIETATIS·CAUSSA·P·C

BASILEA

118

119

123

124

Viterbo cathedral, lying full length, head resting on a cushion. Pope John XXII (XX) is wearing the two-tiered tiara that was then customary. It is one of those statues that does not go beyond the official function of its subject. It scarcely gives any idea of the person whom Dante included among the Fathers of the Church whom he put into his *Divine Comedy*.

VIENNE

"THERE is much that I find irksome here. It is exceptionally cold, and at my age that is not good. The small town is thronged with a great number of people, causing considerable inconvenience." Thus did Raimund, Bishop of Valencia, write in November 1311 to King James I of Aragon. He was writing from Vienne in the Dauphiné. One can well understand the old man. Vienne is on the Rhône and many of its winter days are such as might well be a trial to a man from the sunny coasts of Spain, while the town itself is still small and confined. Heaven alone knows what induced Pope Clement V to convene the Fifteenth General Council there.

Away from the street carrying the through traffic from nearby Lyons to the Riviera, Vienne does not seem either small or confined. The temple of Augustus and Livia can stand comparison with the buildings of imperial Rome. The Church of Saint Maurice does honour to its proud designation of primate's church. Vienne had a good name in the Roman Empire. Diocletian promoted it to the dignity of provincial capital. In the fifth century it was the headquarters of the commander of the Rhône fleet. Its textile factories and potteries provided a sound economic basis for its well-being. The Emperor Claudius in the Senate once praised the men of Vienne, who had deserved well of the state, and the Roman poet Martial said: "If the current report is true, beautiful Vienne is enthusiastic about my work." The city retained its importance. In 1119, Callistus II, the pope of the First Lateran Council, elevated its archbishop to primate of Gaul. It was then assumed that the see, which could be traced back to 314, was the oldest in Gaul. The archbishop of Vienne and primate of Gaul was also lord of the town and country, until the heir to the throne of France disputed his suzerainty, claiming it for himself as Dauphin of Vienne.

The old suspension bridge leading to Place Saint Maurice is bold and picturesque. The square, oblong between its nineteenth-century houses,

66

is dominated by the stone mass of the primate's church, in whose façade   *70*
three tall doorways lead into the interior. They are overloaded with
figures and ornamental carving. The centre of the façade above them is
dominated by a wide window, on either side of which are heavy towers
that now have lost their spires. The stone of their maltreated bodies has
weathered and is returning to its natural state. This is not the façade
that looked down on the Council fathers of 1311. It was built at the end
of the fourteenth and during the fifteenth century, and its upper part
was only completed in 1532. But the three-aisled interior, plain and
simple after the ostentation of the late Gothic façade, did witness the
opening of the Fifteenth General Council on October 16, 1311. The
Council fathers assembled in the central nave. Many of the bishops who
had the right to attend, did not do so, because the Pope, Clement V,
had had to submit the list of those to whom invitations were going out
to the King of France, and any who were not acceptable to Philip the
Fair were not invited. None the less, there were bishops and archbishops
from Spain, England, France, Germany and Italy there, as were the
patriarchs of Alexandria and Antioch, who were given seats of honour
in the middle of the cathedral. As the Council fathers were assembled,
Pope Clement V entered with a small suite and seated himself on the
old bishop's seat that is still there in the centre of the semicircular wall
of the choir. From there he announced the council's programme. This
included the proceedings against the Templars, the recovery of the
Holy Land, reform of morals and piety, and a discussion of the freedom
of the Church.

We can imagine the scene with Clement V on the throne of the archbishops of Vienne, for Andrea da Firenze has painted it in his murals in
the Spanish Chapel of Santa Maria Novella. We have already met this
artist and his work in connection with the Second Council of Lyons. He   *65*
included in that a picture of Saint Thomas Aquinas. Pope Clement V
appears with Thomas Aquinas in the murals devoted to the triumph of
Saint Thomas. He is sitting at the feet of Canonical Law, depicted as a
tall woman holding the church building in her left hand, her right being   *71*
raised as though in the act of instruction. Clement V's hand is raised in
the same gesture, while his left holds Peter's giant key. A red chorister's
mantle falls smoothly from his slight shoulders, held in place by a huge
clasp. On his head he has the triple crown, which he actually wore at

Vienne. Whether it was he or one of his predecessors who added the third crown, is not known, but the addition does not seem to have made him happy. His face appears smooth and cold, and there is a sullen expression about his mouth. His eyes are narrow and mistrustful.

Clement V came from Gascony. He was archbishop of Bordeaux. As Pope he had greatness and an universal breadth of outlook. He realized that the idea of the crusade had had its day. From then on Christendom was not to send soldiers against the heathen, but missionaries. Thus the Council of Vienne decided to set up chairs of Greek, Hebrew and Arabic in the universities of the West. Priests with a mastery of these languages, were then to be sent to work as missionaries to the Jews and Mohammedans in the Near and Far East. The Council appointed the first Archbishop of Pekin. Dante, who did not consign the great men of this world to his hell as indiscriminately as many readers suppose, considered Clement V to have been worse than Boniface VIII. "For after him came ere long from the West a worse, an unbridled spiritual shepherd." Dante condemns Clement V because he disdained Rome and made Avignon the permanent residence of the Popes, and he cursed him as the murderer of the Knights Templar. Andrea da Firenze seemed to have repeated Dante's judgment in his portrait, though he did not nourish romantic dreams of empire, as Dante did, in fact he was sober rather than emotional, cold instead of exuberant, and always clear-headed. The expression he has given this face is that of a man who knows nothing of the happiness of being blessed, of the Pope who at the Council of Vienne approved the most wicked state mass murder in history. King Philip IV, called the Fair (1268–1314), the strong man behind the events of the Council, is depicted in a contemporary minia-ture as a minnesinger with a taste for the chase. Wrapped in a cloak,
73 patterned with the lily from his coat of arms, he is seated affectedly on a bench. It is impossible to tell whether the creatures on either side of him are lions or hounds. On his right and left sit his Queen, Joanna of Navarre, and their sons and daughters. Philip towers above them. He has more hair and a bigger crown than the others, for the artist has been at pains to preserve the general concept of regality, though he seems to have copied the true features of the man who was Philip the Fair. One could well believe a man with this small, coldly brutal mouth capable of the outrage of October 13, 1307. In the night of October 12 he had

the castles and houses of the Templars occupied and the knights themselves arrested. The Order of the Knights Templar, founded in 1119,
had fought for the Church and the West in the Holy Land against the
Saracens, in Spain, fighting against the Moors, and at Liegnitz against
the Mongols. After the loss of the Holy Land, the Knights with the red
cross on their white cloaks had no martial mission left, but they were not
so demoralized as Philip the Fair made out. He was not concerned with
disciplining the Order, but with laying his hands on its vast wealth; so,
in order to obtain this, he tortured and murdered the captured knights
and sent their grand master to the scaffold. Clement, who was dependent
on the king, had to bring the case against the knights before the Council.
Although the case was investigated by a special commission, the Council
fathers could not be prevailed upon to pass sentence, and Clement
found himself constrained to take the responsibility upon himself. He
dissolved the Order by a decree dated March 22, 1312, but he did not
dare to grant its assets to the Knights of Saint John, as the king
demanded. Instead, the French king confiscated their possessions for the
Crown. The dissolution of the Order of the Knights-Templar was
announced at the second session of the Council of Vienne, on April 3,
1312.

The Church of Saint Maurice in Vienne, where this drama was
enacted, is one of the biggest cathderals in the South of France: its
three-naved basilica with chapels of ease in the side aisles was put up in
the twelfth century. In the fourteenth and fifteenth centuries the archbishops lengthened the structure on the west side and completed it with
a late Gothic façade. The twelfth-century structure is typically that of a
cathedral: the pointed arches, pillars surrounded with half-columns, *74, 75*
pillared breaks in the wall-bands of the triphoria lying between the
arches and the windows of the central nave. Ribs give the vaulting
elasticity and elegance. None the less, the interior gives the impression of
being more confined and heavy than that of nearby Lyons cathedral
and you can see that it is older. In the side aisles you will see that on the
heads of the pillars there is much plastic life of animal and human
figures, and although these are some of the best twelfth-century stone-
carving there is in France, it remains of marginal interest. This cathedral is pure architecture. It forms an interior that is high and mighty,
but simple, a suitable place for the Council at its last session of May 6,

1312, to debate the precept of poverty of the Order of Franciscans. It did not oppose the exhortation to the sons of Saint Francis to observe their rules more strictly, but rather pointed out what greatness came from renunciation.

There are no depictions of the Council of Vienne, apart from the final session that is portrayed in one of the murals in the Salone Sistina of the Vatican Library and shows Clement V sitting in an idealized baroque interior in the midst of the Council Fathers. Before him kneels a prelate, who is handing him a book. This represents the acceptance of the reform decrees which were later incorporated in the ecclesiastical code and are important supplements to it.

PISA–CONSTANCE

IN 1409, there were two Popes simultaneously claiming to be the rightful successors of Saint Peter the Apostle. In Rome reigned Gregory XII (1406–1445), a Venetian, and in Avignon Benedict XIII, a Spaniard. All attempts to reach an arrangement between them came to nothing. So, in January 1409, thirteen cardinals decided to convene a general council in order to remove the dangerous schism of this split in the papacy. The place chosen for the Council to meet was Pisa, and no more worthy setting for the Sixteenth General Council *76* could have been found for its cathedral, baptisterium and Leaning Tower give Pisa what is still one of the most splendid church squares in Europe. The Pisans call it Piazza dei Miracoli, the Square of Miracles. Here you get an extensive green, on which dew sparkles in the morning. It is ringed with walls and buildings and on it three marble buildings lie like jewels. They are in fact oblations, donated by the people of Pisa in thanks for the naval victory over the Saracens at Palerno in 1063. *78* Buscheto, one of those eleventh-century architects who tried to compete with the ancient Romans, built a five-naved hall of fame, using the Romans' favourite material, marble, from nearby Carrara, and the decorative forms of Rome and Byzantium, even including some of Saracen origin, on its walls and pillars. Buscheto's successors lengthened the cathedral in the twelfth century and crowned the crossing with a cupola. Four ranks of arches, gleaming and finely worked, were placed in front of the portal side, and, in the fourteenth century, the cupola over the crossing received the crown of a colonnaded gallery of pointed arches.

In 1174, they began building the Leaning Tower. Six pillared galleries ringed the cylinder of the tower, the foundations of which tilted while it was being built. Power and elegance combined in a hovering balance of forces. Opposite the front of the cathedral is the most beautifully preserved baptistery of Christendom. The architect,

Diotisalvi, started work on its round structure in 1153. Between 1260 and 1285 Pisani gave it the chaplet of its dwarf Roman gallery that rings it half-way up, and the fourteenth century saw the addition of the cupola that rests on mighty antique columns.

The Piazza dei Miracoli served the religious needs of the living, but the dead were not forgotten, and, in 1278, a *camposanto* was built for them near by. Gigantic marble halls form cloisters for the dead, the walls of which were decorated with murals by Pisan painters, which are famous in the history of medieval Italian art.

This great gift of the citizens of Pisa provided a sensible setting for the first civil Council of the Church's history. All previous Councils had been convened by emperors or popes, but the invitations to the Council of Pisa went out from cardinals who were adherents of neither Pope nor Emperor, and whose actions were not the arbitrary result of a sudden impulse, but the logical implementation of the so-called conciliar theory, according to which the General Council of the Church had power and authority over all members of the Church, even the Pope. More than a hundred bishops, some two hundred abbots, a hundred deans of chapters and thirteen universities accepted the invitation, and the Council, which was constituted in the cathedral on March 25, 1409, acted as the highest instance of the Church. It called the two popes, Benedict XIII and Gregory XII, to appear before its court, and, when they did not appear, deposed them and elected a Franciscan, Peter Philarghi, who was a Greek and cardinal archbishop of Milan, as the new Pope. He took the name of Alexander V, but died the following year, when his place was taken by a former condottieri and papal legate, Baldassare Cossa of Bologna, who, as John XXIII (XXII) was the Pope of the Council of Pisa. Since neither Benedict nor Gregory had any intention of giving up their papal office, the Church now had three Popes, which caused the chroniclers to remark that instead of "mad dualism" there was now an "accursed trinity".

The central figure of the Council of Pisa was the absent Gregory XII. At his election it had been arranged that he would resign if ever the anti-pope, Benedict XIII, was prepared to do so; but when it came to it and Benedict XIII was prepared to abdicate, Gregory let his supporters persuade him to remain in office, and this was the prime reason behind the Council of Pisa. Girolamo Muziano (1528–1590) has put

129

132

133

134

Pope Gregory into a picture that is now in the Vatican Museum. He is   *77*
depicted seated in an armchair, a purple cloak round his shoulders over
a white robe. His red *cappa* is on his head. He has been reading and is
still holding the book in his left hand. His head is bowed pensively, and
the attitude and expression of his hands repeat what the meditating face
tells us. The room in which the Pope is meditating has a green curtain
and dark brown panelling. It is a narrow room and there is something
liberating about the view through the window, part of which is cut off
by the frame. When Muziano painted his picture, Gregory had been
dead for a hundred and fifty years, but even so he has caught the
character and destiny of his subject. The small face mirrors the indeci-
sion and perplexity of his character. The frame chosen for the picture is
far too pompous for it, just as the papal office was far too much for its
subject. Indeed, Gregory renounced it in 1415 and reverted to being
plain Cardinal Angelo Correr.

All the paintings and other records assembled in Pisa cathedral were
destroyed in a fire in 1595. There is no longer so much as an inscription
to commemorate the Council in this splendid and yet stern interior,
where Roman columns carry the layers of black and white masonry and   *78*
a flat roof. Even so, the visitor is strangely reminded of the events of this
sixteenth general assembly of the church, for, against one of the walls in
the right-hand section of the transept, is the tomb of the Emperor
Henry VII. He was the first Duke of Luxemburg to be Emperor, and it
was at this tomb of his that a Pope was elected who was to help one of
his descendants to the same imperial crown, a man very like him in
manner and spirit. The King of Hungary, Sigismund of this house of
Luxemburg, was one of the first princes to recognize John XXIII
(XXII) as Pope, and when a new Emperor was being chosen in 1410
and the German Electors were hesitating between Jost von Böhmen and
Sigismund, Pope John decided for the King of Hungary. This give-and-
take relationship continued. Sigismund regarded the Hussites of
Bohemia as a threat to his lands and to the unity of the Church, and
John XXIII (XXII) was looking for some means of digging the ground
from under the feet of his two anti-popes; thus, when the two met in
Lodi, Sigismund had little difficulty in arousing the Pope's enthusiasm
for the idea of a Council. John obtained Sigismund's promise of general
recognition, and on October 30, 1414, the Emperor announced this to

the Christian world of East and West. A few weeks later, on December 9, John XXIII (XXII) invited those entitled to attend to come to Constance. The Council of Pisa never having legally been closed, at the Pope's suggestion the sessions in Constance were regarded as a continuation of the sixteenth general assembly that had been opened in Pisa.

On Christmas Eve, 1414, a ship put out from Uberlingen on Lake Constance. It had on board King Sigismund and his retinue. He stepped ashore again in Constance at the great *Kaufhaus* to the sound of Christian bells. He may have been wearing the fur cap in which Konrad Leib of Pisanello has portrayed him. It was certainly a fine
79 useful headgear for that time of year with big flaps to protect his neck and ears. The soft brown of the fur borrows light from the king's fair hair and beard. You can see that the artist has been at pains to reproduce the individuality of the fur. He has been equally painstaking with the king's face, which is turned slightly to the right, making the aquiline nose stand out to better effect. His beautiful, melancholy eyes look past you, and yet there is nothing abstracted about their gaze. The mouth is finely moulded and obviously familiar with the delights of this earth. The parted lips reveal two rows of faultless teeth. The cheek-bones are delicately formed. An air of greatness brings the whole face together, which is one of a man of the world with an universal spirit. This portrait used to be attributed to the Bohemian painter Konrad Leib, but now it is considered to have been the work of Antonio Pisano (Pisanello). Both were masters of early portrait-painting. The portrait brings together all the information about Sigismund that is scattered boringly in the old books and documents. Sigismund was a clever, spirited man of the world, assured in playing politics, heedless in battle, a diplomat and an artist in living. Though the *nouveaux riches* of the fifteenth century made fun of this impecunious wanderer and his continual borrowing, writers and women loved him, because he was indeed a king.

At this time Constance was a free city of the Empire and a bishop's see, and it must have looked very much as represented in the plan of it
80 made in 1600. This lovely water-coloured pen drawing is today in the Rosgarten Museum. It gives a bird's-eye view of the city. Two sides are surrounded by the waters of the lake and the Rhine; the landward side is protected by a wall and towers. From the highest ground in the city

rises the bishop's cathedral, that later became the Minster of Our Lady. Basically it has the same shape as the present structure. Constance *81* was a diocese by 600 and its first cathedral is said to have been built on the masonry of a Roman fort. Hermann the Lame records that Bishop Lambert (995–1015) pulled it down and enlarged it. The new structure had no stability, however, and collapsed in 1052. Bishop Gebhard III built better. His cathedral, which was completed in 1089, still provides *82, 83* the best part of Constance Minster. The north tower was added in the twelfth century, the south tower in the fourteenth. To envisage the structure that housed the Council, you must imagine it without its Gothic, which is all of later addition. In 1414 there were no big Gothic windows to let light into the side-aisles and choir. The central nave had no vaulted roof; that was put in in 1680. At the time of the Council the roof was flat as was customary on basilicas with rounded arches. The three-naved basilica with its east transept has something of the balance between heaven and earth which constituted the happiness of the people of the twelfth century. The slightly tapering pillars, hewn from single blocks of stone, have unusual octagonal capitals ringed with deeply-carved shields. The columns march masterfully and protectingly towards transept and choir. The iconoclasts of the Reformation re-moved all the altars, vessels, pictures and movable statues; but even so there is no lack of pictorial records of the Council that had its sessions there, for one of the burghers of Constance, Ulrich Richental (1437) had the happy idea of keeping a diary of the events, the feasts and all the bustle and life of his town that overnight had become the navel of the world. He recruited some painters and draughtsmen to illustrate his text. The result was a pictorial history that had no lack of readers. In the fifteenth century it was always being copied. The early printing presses helped to popularize it, woodcuts taking the place of its hand-painted illustrations. The original appears to have been lost in a fire at Salem Monastery, but nine copies and prints have been preserved. The Rosgarten Museum possesses not only a printed copy with black-and-white illustrations and another with coloured woodcuts, but, most precious of all, a manuscript of the chronicle, dated 1460, the pictures in which are far superior to any of the others.

Ulrich Richental's picture stories include a "session of the Prelates of *84* the Church in the Minster". Although the architecture is only just indicated, one's eye is struck by the octagonal capitals of the pillars, which are unmistakable. The Pope thrones it in the middle of the semicircle of Council Fathers, tiara on his head. He has a cardinal on either side of him, then bishops with their secretaries squatting at their feet. The speakers taking part in the discussion stand in two pulpits opposite each other.

When King Sigismund reached Constance on Christmas Eve, the Pope was already there, having opened the Council in the cathedral on November 5, 1414. This, too, Ulrich Richental has described and illustrated. You see John entering the city. The old condottieri sits his horse as though he were going in to battle. Then you see him at his *85* height presenting King Sigismund with the golden rose. Ever since the eleventh century these roses were consecrated by the Pope on the fourth Sunday in Lent and presented to deserving recipients as an honour and distinction. Here, Pope John is standing beside the altar, on which his tiara stands, wearing his white mitre. Sigismund is kneeling, bareheaded, while one of his suite holds his crown. The retinues of both Pope and Emperor are made up of bishops and prelates. Everyone's attention is on the Pope, who is in the act of putting the rose in Sigismund's upstretched hands.

"*Joanes Quoram Papa*", "John formerly Pope," is the wording on the marble shroud that two sorrowing angels hold, and the figure that lies on the sarcophagus is that of a Renaissance prince of the church, wearing the mitre and vestment of a cardinal. He is Baldassare Cossa, formerly a Neapolitan mariner, then a dreaded condottieri, a not unsuccessful lawyer, then legate from Bologna; in 1402 he became cardinal and in 1410 Pope, as John XXIII (XXII), dying in Florence in 1419. *86* The city gave him an honoured place in the baptistery, and Donatello, the greatest sculptor of the fifteenth century, made his tomb. The good fortune he had at Constance did not stay with him long. Shortly after the Council started, it decided that thenceforth voting would be by nations, not by heads. That cost John his majority and doubts concerning his conduct finally destroyed all his hopes of being confirmed by that Council. On March 20 he fled in disguise to Schaffhausen, thinking that without a pope the Council would dissolve, but nothing of the sort happened. The Council meted out to John the same fate as his opponent had suffered at Pisa. On May 29, 1415, the "General Synod assembled in the Holy Ghost" deposed John as a "stubborn schismatist, unworthy in manners and belief".

In death, John, formerly Pope, is not wearing the tiara, but Donata di Nicolo di Betto Bardi, known as Donatello (1388–1466) has made up for this by giving him a tomb that leaves those of his competitors for Saint Peter's chair far behind. Two lions, symbols of the law, support his bier, over the edge of which falls a brocade cover. A ceremonial cushion pillows his head. He is wearing the vestment, mitre, gloves and shoes of a cardinal. At this time Donatello had begun working in bronze, and his delight in his new, workable material has lent wings to his hand. The cushion bulges beneath the weight of the head, the robe is crisply silken round the arms. All is alive and forceful. In the fine naturalistic way of the early Renaissance even the ornaments on vestments and mitre are accurately depicted. But it is the expression of the face that shows what Donatello is really capable of. Who else could have interpreted it all so well? In death, the powerful, well-cut features have come to rest, yet still you have the mariner, the soldier, the lawyer, all are depicted here. But the cardinal, the Pope? It is difficult to say whether this man has faith and piety. John's is the characteristic Italian face of his century, beyond good and evil. Beauty it acquired only in death or in art.

Men of this kind take their destiny upon themselves. When John XXIII (XXII) was a prisoner at Radolfzell after his flight, he did what the Council wanted and renounced his office and dignity. Church historians consider that the time when the Council of Vienne was held was on the boundary between two epochs. By Constance, the Middle Ages and modern times were indeed face to face. You can see that when you consider the man who accepted John's abdication, Theobald de Rougemont. He was Archbishop of Besançon and one of the Pope's French opponents. Because of his office and attitude, the Council elected to send him to the prisoner of Radolfzell. He, the archbishop, died in Rome ten years after his papal opponent, and his plaque in the grotto of Saint Peter's has resisted the destructive forces of the centuries, so that he still stands there beneath his Gothic canopy, wearing vestment and mitre, hands crossed below the coat of arms of Besançon that is on his chest. Its eagle, topped by a cross, is repeated in the lateral gables of the canopy. The inscription is a wish that the deceased's

87

"soul may rest in Abraham's bosom". Everything about this sculpture is medieval: inscription, canopy, coats of arms, it all contradicts the spirit of the tomb that Donatello made for the Pope ten years earlier, where a prince lies on his bed of honour, free and great. Here, a very anxious mortal is presented in mere flat relief. In the archbishop's face there is none of the faith or virtue for which the chroniclers praised him. Nor does it have that consciousness of greatness that Donatello has given the Pope. Theobald de Rougemont's ugly features reflect only the narrow-mindedness and cosmic fear that convulsed France and Germany as the fifteenth century progressed.

Where this fear gained the upper hand, it kindled fires at the stake, and of this too Ulrich von Richental's chronicle has a tale to tell. The pages for July 1415 include a picture of two bishops depriving a priest of his vestments. "Hus is divested of his clerical garments," is the inscription. John Hus (1369–1415), son of a Czech peasant, was a theologian and twice rector of Prague University. He was one of those reformers who refused to accept the principle of any temporal organization of the Church. Like John Wyclif (1330–1384) he regarded the church as a spiritual community of those predestined for salvation. The Council of Constance condemned Wyclif's teachings on May 4, 1415. Hus's defence was: "I teach no error, no Czech is a heretic." As he refused to recant, he too was condemned as a heretic on July 6, 1415, and deprived of his clerical office. The next picture in the chronicle shows Hus in the garb of a heretic, a long black gown and a large cap on which two devils with tails cavort. The text says that Hus is being led to the place of execution. The soldiery accompanying him leave no doubt about this. That Hus had come to Constance only because King Sigismund had given him a safe conduct was disregarded. According to Dietrich von Nien, an official in the papal chancellery and a writer who was an untiring "herald of the glories of the Emperor in the Late Middle Ages", a safe conduct had no validity where a heretic was concerned. Sigismund acted in accordance with the lights of his day when he sent Hus to the stake. Richental's chronicle shows him "on the burning pyre", saying to his executioners "I die joyfully for the Gospel". Two henchmen are tending the flames with great forks, while soldiers, burghers and priests look on. Is the young man to the left and behind the bowed executioner the humanist Poggio, who was Pope John's secretary at the Council? He was present and wrote in his diary that Hus was *"vir praeter fidam egregius"*, apart from his beliefs a distinguished man. The flames seem to have done their work thoroughly, for in the next picture two gallows-birds are busy shovelling a heap of ash into a baby hangman's cart. "The ashes were carted away and strewn in the Rhine," Ulrich Richental remarks laconically.

Sigismund's action in letting Hus be publicly burned was in accordance with the spirit of the age, but even so the death of Hus, the heretic, seems to have been politically advantageous to him as well. Hus spoke and wrote Czech and his adherents were mainly from the Czech lower classes. They wanted to set up "The Kingdom of God in Bohemia". Inspired by the idea that the Czechs were Christ's chosen people on earth, they were in revolt against the Germans. Sigismund considered that his house's basic territories were in danger. Unfortunately, when he realized that political problems cannot be solved at the stake, it was too late. The flames that burned Hus kindled the conflagration of the Hussite war, which was to put King Sigismund's realm in mortal danger.

When John XXIII (XXII) fled, it caused a panic. Eight cardinals and many other Council Fathers left the city; the itinerant merchants packed up their wares and the Burgomaster mobilized the city militia. King Sigismund proved master of the situation. Accompanied by the Count-Palatine, Ludwig, he rode through the agitated city and "continually had it proclaimed to all money-changers, whether Italians or others, to all traders and merchants, to all cardinals and lords, calling out himself in his own voice that nobody was to leave", so says the trusty Ulrich Richental, who recounts the event in words and pictures. Sigismund was able to control the panic in the city, but he was unable to cure the shock the Pope's flight inflicted on Christendom. People saw their hopes of unity and reform in the Church abruptly dashed. After the abdication of John XXIII (XXII), Gregory XII and Benedict XIII contended for Saint Peter's throne. Gregory had both vision and magnanimity. He convened the Council again and on July 4, 1415, tendered his own resignation. Benedict XIII, however, stubbornly refused to give up his office, even though King Sigismund undertook a special journey to Narbonne to try and persuade him to resign. On the king's return on July 26, 1417, the Council again deposed Benedict.

79

By the treaty of Narbonne Sigismund had managed to get some of Benedict's supporters, including the kings of Aragon, Navarre, Castile and Portugal, to withdraw their support from him. The Council then 95 hastened to elect a new pope. The Conclave met on November 8.

Beside the lake is an impressive building which the people of Constance call "the Council Building" or just "the Council". It was built in 1388–1404 by Heinrich Arnott to house that department of the city's administration in charge of trade and traffic. It was also used for ceremonial occasions, and kings and emperors have danced with the ladies 96 of Constance in its hall. The city plan of 1600 shows a massive two-storeyed building. The ground floor has wide cross-windows and a round-arched doorway. This is now hidden by the terrace built in front of it, but the upper storey with its close row of little windows is still as it was in 1600. Inside there are two halls, one above the other, divided into three aisles by oak pillars with cubical capitals. They are roofed with a mighty hip-roof that is a masterpiece of the carpenters' craft.

Despite its name, the building was never used by the Council, though the Conclave met in it on November 8, 1417. This consisted of the cardinals and six delegates from each nation at the Council. Ulrich Richental has recorded how those who were to elect the pope entered in solemn procession, and how a wooden hoarding then shut the building off from the rest of the world, while the keys were taken charge of by the Grand Master of Rhodes. Armed guards searched even the food that was brought for those inside. The election arrangements decided on by the Council of Vienne were adopted and, on November 11, a Roman Cardinal, Otto Colonna, received the tiara. According to Ulrich Richental, earlier that day two votes were still needed for the two-thirds majority, but when the burghers of Constance marched past in a rogatory procession with the boys' choir singing *"Veni creator spiritus,"* the sound of which was like an admonition in the ears of the cardinals, two of them, moved to tears, voted for Colonna, so that, before the cross at the head of the procession had got back to the minster, the people in the streets were crying out: "We have a pope, Otto of Colonna."

Otto Colonna (1368–1431) chose the name of Martin V, and was crowned in the minster of Constance, while visitors and burghers rejoiced. One of Richental's illustrators has recorded the historical

146

HERCVLES GONZAGA MANTVAN · HIER° SERIPANDVS NEAP · STANISLAVS POLONVS · LVDOVICVS
SIMONETT MEDIOLANE · MARVS SITICVS D ALT EPS GIERMAN · CAROLVS A LOTARINGIA GALVS · LVDOVI
CVS MALVVTIVS ELEC EPS TRID · ANTONI ARCHIEPS PRAGEN ORAT C C S PREG BOHE GEORGI EPS
ORAT CÆ PREGE HVG · VALENTINVS EPS PREMISCIE ORAT REGIS POLONIÆ · M ANTONI EPS AVGVSTA
····· VS SABAVDI · SIGISMVNDVS AT VN ORAT C ÆSAREVE · LVDOVICVS LANNAC ORAT REGIS
····· FERDINAND MARTINEZ ORAT REGIS PORTVGALI · NICOLAVS DE PONT ORAT TVM ·····
·········· A IN EMORA ····· N · MATCHIOL VISIO ORAT · HEVVETIE · · QVES PROCOLCO ····
LORENTI · ARGENVS EM KEL ··· IN SEINE BARI CONC · ÆCLA DE OMES TVNE ORAT AC REGIS HISPANI ··

DOM

DEIPARÆ SEMPER VIRGINI IMMACULATÆ CONCEPTÆ, SANCTIS ANGELIS CUSTODIBUS, DIVO VIGILIO PATRONO,
ET ALIIS SANCTIS EPISCOPATUS TRIDENTINI DEFENSORIBUS, AC ALIIS OMNIBUS. PUBLICATIO SS GENERALIS ET
OECUMENICI CONCILII TRIDENTINI IN HOC INSIGNI ET PERVETUSTO TEMPLO CATHEDRALI FACTA 3 &4 XBRIS 1563.
EX VOTO

OB LIBERATIONEM HUIUS CIVITATIS AB OBSIDIONE GALLORUM, ET CONIURATORUM SECUTAM 8. 7BRIS 1703.
CAROLI FERDINANDI S.R.I. COMITIS, LODRONI, ET CASTRI ROMANI TUNC GUBERNATORIS, DOMINI CASTRORUM S. IOANNIS, NOVI
CASTELLANI, ERENTRAIS, GAMUNDII, PIBERSTEIN, HIMELBERG, SUMMEREG, WOLCHENSDORFF, LAMPEDING, PIGNORATITII
RATEMBERGII, MARESCHALLI HÆREDITARII SALISBURGI, LATERANI, PATRITII ROMANI, NOBILIS UNGARIÆ,
CANONICI, PREPOSITI ECCLESIÆ CATHEDRALIS, ARCHIPRESBYTERI VILLÆ, VALLIS LAGARINÆ, PRIORIS GENERALIS
SCHOLARUM DOCTRINÆ XANÆ, & OLIM VICARII GEN

S CRUCIFIXUS, ANTE CUIUS PEDES SUBSCRIPTUM FUIT S.CONCIL. II. CARDINALES LEGATI, ET ALII.III. ORATORES
ECCLIT. IV. ORATORES SECULARES V. ORATOR REGIS HISPANIARUM VI PATRIARCHÆ. VII. ARCHIEPISCOPI.
VIII. EPISCOPI. IX. ABBATES X. GENERALES XI. DOCTORES LEGUM THEOLOGI PONTIFICII, REGUM GALLIÆ
ET CATHOLICI PORTUGALLIÆ ET DUCIS XII. PROCURATORES EPISCOPORUM ABSENTIUM. XIII
ROCURATORES ORDINUM XIV THEOLOGI SECULARES ET DOCTORES IURIS CANONICI THEOLOGI
EDITIONI PRÆDICATORUM DE OBSERVANTIA MINORUM CONVENTUALIUM
AUGUSTIN CARMELITÆ ET COMISSARIUS XVI SECRETARIUS XVII
NOTARII XVII SORES

PAVLO·III
FARNESIO·PONT
OPT·MAX

moment, when the rightful Pope is receiving the tiara. In the foreground is the cathedral choir, singing; above the heads of the choir Martin V can be seen seated on the simple bishop's throne, already clad in the *90* papal vestments. He has folded his hands, and two cardinals and the Grand Master of Rhodes are placing the tiara on his head.

The Pope was worthy of the popular jubilation over his election. Son of a princely Roman house, he had lived a simple, pious life. He was clever and resolute, yet ready to take the advice of those who knew, and these virtues stood him in good stead in Constance. The Council had tested the papal authority severely. The conciliar theory had triumphed with the decree of April 6, 1415, that begins with the word "Sacrosancta". This laid it down that any Christian, even the Pope, owed the Council obedience in matters of faith, ecclesiastical unity and reforms of head and members. The decree "Frequens" of October 9, 1417, took this conception a step further, making the Council an institution meeting at regular intervals and a permanent check on the Pope. Martin V took a different view of the papal office and thanks to his personality he earned it new respect, even in Constance.

That he was able to increase the standing of the papal office is shown by the very fact of his being buried in Christendom's place of honour, Saint John Lateran, the chief and mother church of Rome and the *45–48* whole world. He lies buried there before the altar, the canopy of which venerates the heads of Saint Peter and Saint Paul. The author of his bronze plaque is not known. There is nothing artistically great about its *91* ornamental frame: lines of acanthus leaves serve as a frieze, there is no life in the tendrils then depicted with stereotyped exactitude. Even the folds of the Pope's robe are mean and far too many. The whole seems to be an expression of the spirit that made a mockery of the Council's desire to introduce reforms, for those actually decided upon at Constance were as general and formal as their design. They concerned the choice of bishops and abbots, benefices and indulgences and the dues that had to be paid to the curia in Rome, when an office was conferred. It is said that, when it came to it, Martin V blocked the great reforms and his tomb would seem to confirm this judgment; but if so, how could he have been "*Temporum suorum felicitas*", the good fortune of his day, as the inscription on his tomb says he was?

Donatello is traditionally supposed to have been asked to express an opinion on the bronze, and the assumption is that he then "creatively remodelled" the face; if that is so, then he has saved the memory of a great man, for the face in its majesty triumphs over the mean maze of shapes by which it is surrounded. The dead man is the only thing on the gravestone that has any life. There are no mean or false features in the face, nor is there any pretence of Caesar-like qualities, as there is in the colossal statue the people of Milan put up to him, because he consecrated the high altar of their cathedral, which they had at last completed. This countenance has a greatness that does not come from office, and it would seem to justify those church historians who maintain that the reforms were not blocked so much by the Pope, as by the wrangling and envy of the Council Fathers.

Another of the illustrations of the Richental Chronicle shows the retinue of a great lord gathered round the big-round-arched portal. The horses are pawing the ground impatiently and the herald's tabards are fluttering in the morning breeze, while a man and a woman look down on the colourful scene from an oriel window. This was April 18, *92* 1417, and the horsemen and servants are waiting for their lord and master, Burgrave Frederick of Zollern, who on that day was enfeoffed with Mark Brandenburg by his friend, King Sigismund. This picture is *94* taken from the copy of part of the Chronicle in the Spencer Collection of New York Public Library which was illustrated by a different artist from that of the Rosgarten copies and dates between 1450 and 1460. The ceremony is taking place in Upper Market. On the left of the picture King Sigismund is seated, crown on his head, orb in his right hand and the standard of his realm in his left. Beside him, on the right, kneels Count Frederick. The group is framed by temporal and ecclesiastical dignitaries, horsemen and trumpeters. It is a noisy, lively scene as it deserves to be, for this is the start of the history of Prussia.

We do not know whether this is an exact copy of the lost manuscript, but the head of King Sigismund at least seems to be a likeness, agreeing *79* with the face on the seal he used in Constance. Here, the king is sitting *97* under a Gothic canopy, the lily sceptre in his right hand and the orb in his left. The narrow face and crown are the same as in the Chronicle's *93* illustration, but the building the illustrator depicts as being the Count's residence is not like that in the Zollern Strasse today.

The Council of Constance was the most important and brilliant event of the first half of the fifteenth century, and between 1414 and 1418 the city of Constance was the centre of the world. To it had come King Sigismund and his envoys, many sovereigns and princes of the West, more than three hundred Council Fathers, cardinals, bishops and abbots and their numerous retinues, while itinerant traders, travellers, writers and artists, players and loafers came pouring in to add to the overcrowding. At the time the city was supposed to have ten thousand inhabitants, which number was trebled by the twenty thousand who came for the Council. How the city housed and fed them, kept order and security is a mystery; but it did. We know from the Richental Chronicles that in the fish market snails and frogs, which the "Welsh" prized so highly, *102* were readily obtainable; while "foreign bakers" helped to meet the vast increase in the demand for bread and cakes. They had transportable *103* bread-ovens mounted in handcarts. In the picture you see cakes being taken out of one of these, and the customers waiting for them. In such a situation fishmongers, bakers and others asked the prices for their wares that they thought they could get, and living became dreadfully dear. One of the last German minnesingers, Oswald von Walkenstein, who was in King Sigismund's retinue, lamented: "When I think of Lake Constance, I am sorry for my purse." But he at least had the good fortune to have rare coins in his purse, not just the ordinary ones of France, Germany and Italy that circulated then, but some of the gold guldens that Pope John XXIIII (XXII) had had specially minted. There is one in the Rosgarten Museum: on the face is Saint Peter with *98, 99* his book and key, and on the reverse the Pope's arms and name.

The medieval building that served the Council in Constance: the minster, Kaufhaus, Hohe Haus and the Upper Market are still there, and others too, such as the Dominican monastery on the island which served as meeting place for two of the nations at the Council, the French and Italians. Though it has been much restored, there is an inscription on a tomb there which contains a reference to the Council. The tomb is that of Chrysoloras, the Byzantine envoy.

King Sigismund's Queen lived during the Council in the Federal Court Building, and he himself stayed for a time in the monastery of the Austin friars. This no longer exists, but Sigismund erected a memorial of his stay in the Church of the Trinity, which used to belong to the *100* friars. This was a cycle of murals, which he had painted on the upper

101 walls of the central nave in 1417. These murals were executed by Heinrich Gürbel, Kaspar Sünder and Hans Lederhoser, and they present life according to the rules of the Order and that of the anchorite. When the church was given a baroque interior, the murals were whitewashed. In 1906 and 1957 they were uncovered again, and now they look rather out of place in the baroque interior, but there is nothing else like them in this part of the world.

BASLE–FERRARA–FLORENCE

"THE morals of the people in Basle, being humans, differ. What they have promised, they keep without remonstrance. They neither steal others' property, nor squander their own; satisfied with what is there, they prefer to be honourable than just to seem it. Thus not unjustly has this town been given the name of Basle, which comes from the Greek and means Queen. Actually, Basle is a Queen, for it now harbours the queen of the church, the sacred assembly of the Council. According to others, the founders and first builders of the city came across an enormous basilisk and the name of Basle comes from that. If that is so, this fits in with the Council quite well; for just as a person who looked at the basilisk was lost, so is a heretic, who merely hears of the Council, done for. But it seems to me most probable that the name comes from the word Basis, because the divine plan envisaged that the general assembly should be held there to fortify the basis of faith and the authority of the church," so wrote the young secretary of the Council, Enea Silvio de Piccolomini in one of his famous letters of 1438. As a humanist he had a sixth sense for the auras of historical places. Five hundred years later people no longer trusted conjecture, but only the archaeologist and his spade. In 1947 a small structure was excavated behind the choir of the Basle minster. It had three vaulted passages, which end towards the Rhine in the round walls of three apses. This was the crypt of a Carolingian basilica, like that in the abbey church of Saint Denis near Paris. Saint Denis was built in the middle of the ninth century. The Basle crypt is older, perhaps because it enjoyed the special favour of the Frankish kings from the early years of Charlemagne? At the beginning of the ninth century, the bishop's throne in Basle was occupied by one of the most important men of the age, Bishop Hatto. He was the Emperor's friend and adviser. Great men and circumstances give rise to great architecture.

History continued to favour the city of Basle, which was a favourite of the Emperor Henry II, the Saint. Work on a new cathedral to replace the Carolingian one had been begun about 1000 by Bishop Adalbero, shortly before Henry II's coronation. Henry made the building his personal concern, and provided money, materials and works of art in profusion, so that later he was regarded as its founder.

Enea Silvio de Piccolomini was right in saying that the Council met on holy ground rendered sublime by great architecture. It was a fitting setting for the seventeenth General Assembly that began its deliberations there on July 23, 1431, having been convened by Pope Eugene IV (1431–1447), the same year that he became pope. Its objects were to introduce reforms, bring the Hussites back into the fold and try to achieve union with the Greek church.

The cathedral in which the three hundred delegates began their discussions under the chairmanship of Cardinal Cesarini was not the same building as had stood in the time of Henry II. That had been destroyed by fire in 1185. The new cathedral and the present one was built by Bishop Henry, Count of Harburg. Lateral chapels of ease were added in 1306 and 1346. Then in 1350 an earthquake shook the city and severely damaged the cathedral. Its great vaulting collapsed, the upper part of the choir and the east towers that encompassed it toppled into the river. Rebuilding had not been finished by the time the Council met. Bishop Johann Senn had had the choir rebuilt quickly, but the repairs to the nave and transept had proved laborious and lengthy, and were not finished till 1401. The building of the north tower by the entrance was not complete until three years after the Council.

104–106 Basle Minster is a late romanesque basilica. Its nave has three aisles, the lateral ones being lower than the central nave, as is the basilica pattern, but they have galleries which provide an upper storey. This gave rise to the three-aisled galleried basilica. A broad transept follows the nave. The choir, which ends in a hexagon, is especially interesting architecturally. Its unknown architect surrounded it with an open arcade, for the first time giving a bishop's church a choir-gallery, at least in the lands where German is spoken. Originally, this was a French idea. The pointed arch, which appeared between the columns of the nave quite early on, originated in Burgundy, and the galleried basilica was a product of the Lower Rhine and Lombardy. The architecture of the cathedral is thus typical of the unity of the Occident that existed in the twelfth century. The architect of Basle Minster drew on several countries and added something of his own to produce what was both local and European. There is power and vastness in the masonry and in the wide span of the ribs of the vaulting. The stones of the columns and walls of the nave have been worked most carefully. The whole cathedral seems to reflect the solid, earth-bound character of the people of Basle.

The minster was a fitting setting for the Council, but the seating seems not to have been thought adequate, for the City Fathers decided in 1432 to have new choir stalls built, and these are still there in the choir and transept. Made of oak and walnut, they have the form and *107–109* ornamentation of late Gothic: three tiered rows set against a wall screened with arcades and tracery. The Late Middle Ages' love of the grotesque and of pictorial allegory is reflected in the fools' heads, adages and heraldic animals on the arm-rests and on the misericords, the buttock-rests on the backs of the upturned seats.

Walking through the Basle minster you realize why, in the fifteenth century, it was for many years the motive centre of the West. If only we had something more than historical imagination to help us envisage the events of the Council and the personalities who attended it, but in the minster there is nothing, and elsewhere all that remains from the time of the Council are the two bronzes now in the Historical Museum.

The destruction wrought by the iconoclasts in 1529 must have been considerably greater than one would imagine from the statues in the so-called Council hall and the two contemporary funerary plaques now in the Historical Museum. Of these two plaques, one is in memory of Hermann Wydelerse, Prior of Neuhausen who died in the city on July 30. He was representing one of the many absent bishops and princes, for many had sent representatives to Basle, as they had to Constance, instead of going themselves.

The second bronze is that of Hugo, Archbishop of Rouen, who died on August 19, 1434 and was buried in the church of Saint Peter in the City. The inscription is not informative and leaves you thinking that here is a laudable exception, an archbishop who personally attended the Council. But Rouen? Hugo of Rouen? Does that not conjure up a picture, a picture of a stake and flames, of Joan of Arc being burned in the market-place of Rouen? That was on May 30, 1431.

87

Archbishop Hugo and the French Council Fathers hurried to Basle immediately after the execution. They had condemned Joan as a heretic because she refused to allow the "Church militant" to assess the extent of the task that she had been given by the "Church triumphant". To Joan, the Archangel Michael and the saints who had commanded her to liberate France were the Church triumphant, while the learned theologians of the court were the "Church militant". In those days university doctors had the say in the Church, and to them her invocation of the Church triumphant was as heretical as her appeal to the Pope. They could not see beyond the controversy and were themselves setting the authority of the Church against that of the Pope in accordance with the conciliar theory developed at Constance. Now, in the winter of 1431, they wanted to do to Pope Eugene IV what they had already done to the Maid of Orleans in Rouen.

The Council of Basle was poorly attended, and when by the late autumn of 1431 many were still not there or even represented, the Pope dissolved the Council. That was on December 18. The Council Fathers who were there, refused to accept this and stayed on. They again promulgated the Constance decree "Sacrosancta", according to which the highest instance in the Church is the Council, not the Pope. The "Church militant" of the fifteenth century threw down the gauntlet to its Pope and summoned him before it, as though before a Court.

Eugene IV could be irresolute, but he was not to be intimidated. He

112, 113 has been well depicted by Isaia da Pisa, who was not a new Phidias, Policletus or Praxiteles as Porcello Pandone tried to make out, but a sculptor with the fine Renaissance gift of comprehending the essentials of his subject's character and conveying them in finest marble, that was also a lifelike representation. He has shown the Pope lying outstretched on his sarcophagus as on a couch. His face is strong, but also pious and kind. The features are those of a self-assured ruler, and Eugene IV was the first of the line of princes and scholars on the throne of Saint Peter which began with the Renaissance. It is not mere chance that Eugene wears the tiara, the triple crown of the Popes, even in death. However, even the Pope as prince needs intercession, and the Virgin and child bend towards him, while angels kneel on either side. The Pope of the Second Great Council of Reform had more need than others of the help of the Church Fathers, and there, in the niches the sculptor has made

IOANNES CALVINVS

HÆC ROMANORVM EST FERDINANDI REGIS IMAGO
DA QVISQVIS DEBES HVICQ; DEOQ; SVVM.
M·D· Isl· LVI·

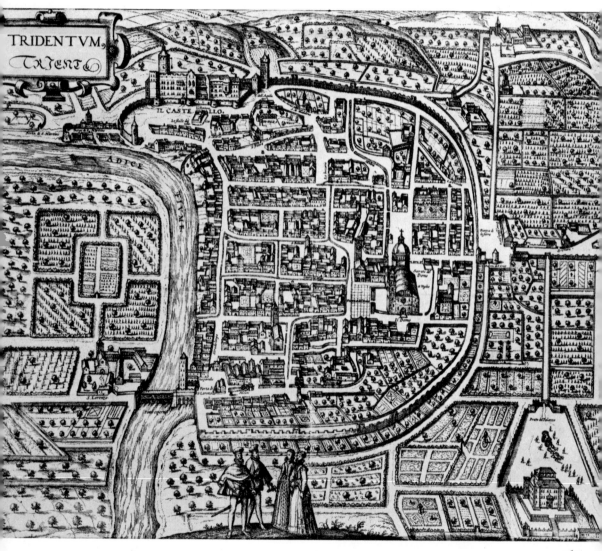

167

in the pillars between which the sarcophagus stands, are Saint Gregory the Great, Saint Jerome, Saint Augustine and Saint Ambrose, while there are cherubs on the lintel that rests on the pillars. The whole is topped by an enormous shell, that used to be the symbol of eternity. Sarcophagus and pillars are set on a tall pedestal on which is an inscription flanked by the Pope's coat of arms, that of the Condulmiere, an aristocratic family of Venice. For half a century this tomb acted as a model, for with it began that style of Roman sculpture that was soon to be known as Renaissance. It was then in an aisle of the old basilica of Saint Peter and, when that was demolished, it was transferred to the Monastery of San Salvatore in Lauro.

The masterful face on this sarcophagus is not that of a man who would submit tamely, nor did Eugene IV, when he received the Council's summons sixteen years before his death. But he was a man who would accept advice, not that this was always to his own or the Church's advantage, but on this occasion it was. The advice given him was that he ought to come to an understanding with the learned doctors in Basle and get the Council working again. This advice came from Francesca Buzzi, a Roman lady who had founded the Congregation of Oblatus in 1425. Today, Rome does her honour as its favourite saint in the church of Santa Francesca Romana in the Forum, where Giroloamo da Cremona has depicted her along with Saint Benedict and the Madonna in one of the chapels of ease. It is not easy to know whether one is to go by this rather arid portrait by a contemporary or by the sculptured one by Gianlorenzo Bernini executed two hundred years *111* later. A person's spirit and character are not necessarily conveyed in faithful reproduction of the flesh. Under Bernini's hands the marble has acquired life and the coolness of white linen. The face here is so obviously the gateway of the soul and that of a woman whose advice one can well understand a Pope taking.

There is another figure that emerges from the twilight of the early history of the Basle Council, that of the greatest mind of the fifteenth century, Nicolas Krebs of Cues on the river Moselle. He was the son of a boatman and had studied in Heidelberg, Padua and Cologne. When he came to Basle to attend the Council he was thirty-one years old and dean of Saint Florin in Coblenz. He was one of the doctors, the learned theologians, and like his fellows he set the Council higher than the Pope;

but the conflict with Eugene IV scandalized him and made him give considerable thought to the Council's claim and the Pope's own point of view. The result of this was his first important work *De Concordantia Catholica* (*On Catholic Unity*) which appeared in 1433. This endeavour to reconcile the Church's domestic conflict was to stamp his whole life.

116   We have no picture of the Dean of Saint Florin. There is a Nicolas of Cues in the Church of San Pietro in Vincoli in Rome; but this figure kneeling opposite Michaelangelo's Moses, is the old cardinal of that name who died in 1464 in Todi in Umbria. It is the work of Andrea Bregno, another of those sculptors who, like Isaia da Pisa, who made Eugene IV's tomb, put fresh life into hidebound Roman art. To make a tomb that was a monument commemorative of his subject's fame was no difficult task for him; but in making this tomb for Cardinal von Cues in San Pietro in Vincoli he went back to medieval forms. The middle of the marble tablet is occupied by Saint Peter, patron of the church. To the right of him kneels the angel who has removed his chains, and on his left is the cardinal, praying. Thus the central position is not given to the dead man, as it usually is, but to the church's patron. The dead man has to be content with a place at the side, that given to the founder in medieval altars. One can only assume that Andrea Bregno's adoption of this arrangement, which in 1464 was definitely reactionary, was in response to the wishes of the person who commissioned the tomb—or of the cardinal, expressed perhaps in a will, for "the first modern thinker" was also a pious and, for a prince of the church, a very modest man. Whichever it was, there is no other tomb in Rome dating from the same period that pays so little attention to the fame and standing of its occupant. Nicolas von Cues was a theologian and a philosopher, a mathematician and a scientist. His ideas and researches went far beyond the ideas of the world of the Middle Ages. He was more modern than the popes and cardinals, to whom the modern monuments of the early Renaissance were set up.

The contradiction between the cardinal's personality and the reflection of it in his tomb is also evident in the style of the carving. Saint Peter and the angel have been made ordinary formalized figures, but the head of von Cues is obviously a portrait. It has the heavy features you will still see along the Moselle. The nose is strong and prominent, the mouth shut and overshadowed by deep furrows. The eyes and forehead speak of clarity of thought. There is greatness about this face, but also the shadow of the melancholy that comes from knowing, as Socrates did, that in the end we know nothing. You can say that "the first modern thinker" has a modern face. Andrea Bregno was a talented portraitist.

On August 14, 1431, at Taus in Bohemia, the Hussites defeated the force of Crusaders sent against them. The Crusaders' commander, Giuliano Cesarini, narrowly escaped being killed. This was the same Cesarini whose representative opened the Council of Basle on July 23, 1431, and who, thirteen years later, fell in battle against the Turks at Varna in Bulgaria, after which his friends struck a memorial medal in his honour. On this the words, "Julianus Caesarinus" in capital letters *110* frame the profile of a bearded man. The features and expression are big and bold, and even the folds of the robes on the shoulder have something grand about them. Cesarini was no yokel, but one of that generation of "golden youths" born about 1400, who were humanists, studied the writings of the ancient Romans and Greeks and sought in their thoughts, acts and example to bring about a new conception of greatness in art, intellect and behaviour, a renaissance. Giuliano de Cesarini loved the Latin form of his name, Julianus Caesarinus, which sounded like Julius Caesar and the resonance of which lent an air of princely greatness to the little portrait of him on the medal. He was, of course, never a Caesar, but he was a cardinal at the age of twenty-eight and then papal legate on the battlefields of intellect and arms throughout the Holy Roman Empire. The mind and pursuits of the scholar did not stop him being a man of action. In this he resembles his pupil and friend, Nicolas von Cues, and it was the endeavour of both to remove conflict. His moderate policy of negotiation did lead to a compromise between the Council Fathers and the Pope, who withdrew the decree of December, 1433 dissolving the Council.

Early 1433 saw a powerful ally of those, men and women, who wished to continue the Council arrive in Rome. This was Sigismund, who was king at the time of the Council of Constance. Later, in the summer of that year, he landed in Basle, having come by boat from Zurich. According to the chronicle of voll Bürgerstolz, as he stepped ashore, he demanded new shoes, because his own were no longer fit to walk in through the city. Worn though his shoes may have been, he brought with him from Rome the longed for imperial crown. Pope

Eugene IV had crowned him Holy Roman Emperor in Saint Peter's on May 31st. We have a sculpture depicting the ceremony by a contemporary, Filarete.

In 1433, a Florentine sculptor, Antonio di Pietro Averlino, came to Rome. In rather touching modesty he called himself Filarete, friend of virtue, and it is as this that he has a place in the history of art. Eugene IV commissioned him to make bronze doors for Saint Peter's. These were later taken from the old building and used in Moderna's new one, and today they grace the middle door. Filarete divided each half into three fields: on the topmost appear Christ, Mary and Saints Peter and Paul, and the two middle fields depict the martyrdom of the apostles. Artistically much more important than these big reliefs are the rails, the surfaces with which Filarete separated them. In these he tells about the Council, becoming as Leo Bruhus wrote in his *Art in the City of Rome*, "the first reporter of his century".

The main figures on the door seem awkward and heavy, but these reportage reliefs are interesting, fresh and accurate. These masters of the down-to-earth style, that came into being about 1430, obviously felt sure of themselves as soon as they were depicting people and events of their own day, while the imaginative, made-up picture they found difficult. We saw this in the case of Andrea Bregno and the difference between his statue of Nicolas von Cues and the figures of the apostles and angels. Here, Pope Eugene is sitting in front of an altar on which stand a chalice and two candlesticks with lighted candles. He is wearing the tiara and full papal vestments. The Emperor Sigismund is kneeling before him in his coronation cloak. He has already received sword and orb from the Pope, who is now placing the imperial crown on his head. Sigismund has the same long beard that he has in the statues of Conrad Laib and Antonio Pisanello of about 1430. Two bishops are assisting the Pope, and the Emperor's suite stands thronged at a respectful distance. Garlands give a festive air to the act of coronation. Being a good reporter, Filarete has not forgotten his caption, and on the upright part of the frame on the right you can read "INCORONATO IMPERATORIS SIGISMUNDI", Coronation of King Sigismund.

Sigismund hoped that the Basle Council would bring about the downfall of the Hussites, which had seemed imminent at Constance, but which subsequently his forces had been unable to achieve. Now, the heads of the movement appeared in Basle, led by Procopius and a compromise was reached. The church allowed the Hussites to receive the Sacraments as mere bread and wine and made other concessions.

Meanwhile the number of Council Fathers increased. In the words of Hubert Jedin in his *Kleine Konziliengeschichte*: "Whoever was a member of the Council had a vote and could be elected to one or other of the four Committees for General Matters, Dogma, Reform and Peace. The whole was directed by a Management Committee. In the way it did its business, the Council resembled a modern parliament, as also in its tendency to take more and more upon itself and so, perhaps, become the real government of the Church."

This method of working favoured reform, and between 1433–1436 reforms dealing with liturgy, diocesan synods and priest's concubinage were passed. All thus went well until they came to the question of the importance of the papal throne, at which point the Council again came into conflict with Pope Eugene IV, and, when the Council began proposing to deprive the curia of the bulk of its income, a new breach was inevitable. The ostensible cause of the breach was the question whether the Emperor, John VIII, from Constantinople, and the Patriarch Joseph should meet the Council in Basle or some other place. The Council Fathers decided on Basle and the Pope chose Ferrara, and ordered the Council to transfer its seat there on September 18, 1437. A minority did go to Ferrara, among them Cesarini and Nicolas von Cues. The majority, however, remained in Basle, including the third and youngest of the Council's great men, Enea Silvio de Piccolomini (1405–1464). The house of Piccolomini has given the world two popes and a famous general immortalized in Schiller's *Wallenstein*. The charm of this its son, Enea Silvio, captivated his contemporaries. We have many portraits of him. In the Church of San Andrea della Valle in Rome is one of the most pretentious tombs of the Renaissance which is his; but he is seen to the best advantage in the murals by Bernardino di Betto di Biagio, known as Pinturicchio (1502–1508), in the Cathedral Library of Siena, which Pope Pius III, Piccolomini-Todeschini, founded to house the papers and library of his uncle, Enea Silvio, half a century after his death as Pope Pius II, Pinturicchio has not painted his series of murals about this great son of Siena as reportage. They seem rather to be a glorified fairy-tale, and it is very doubtful whether any Sienese of the beginning of the sixteenth century, who happened to have been in the cathedral library and seen the frescoes depicting Enea Silvio's life, would seriously have believed that people or any town in Italy could have looked like that forty years previously. The frescoes depict what even to contemporaries must have been an unreal, impossible countryside in which men and women remained eternally young and handsome, where it was always Sunday and the sky eternally blue and people always wore the most splendid and gorgeous clothes.

Enea Silvio de Piccolomini wrote a deathless love story *Euryalus and Lucretia* and his letters make him the first great travel writer in European literature. He also wrote a history of the Basle Council and a biography of the Emperor—Frederick III, whom he served as Secretary of the Council, following the family tradition. Today, he is regarded as one of the most important scholars and also the greatest Pope of the Renaissance. Only this sort of fairy-tale can do justice to men of this stamp, and thus it is that Enea has found his right portraitist in Pinturicchio. In the

117   first pictures the young humanist is setting out for the Council of Basle; he is shown as a richly dressed youth on a white horse thrusting in to join a company of men on horseback, while he himself has turned his head to look behind him at the beholder. Enea was then secretary of Cardinal Domenico Capranica who, although a man of considerable importance, is here kept in the background, just visible above the white horse's head, but recognizable by his hat. It is a handsome, graceful company. The horses' skins are glossy, weapons glint and colourful clothes glow in the Tuscan sunshine. Was the red ever so warm, the blue so deep or the green so mossy-green? This magnificent scene is shown against a dream landscape. Warships are putting in to an unreal harbour at the foot of cliffs studded with houses. The heavens are being split open by a thunderstorm, but a rainbow is already reaching down to earth with its message of comfort. When man is silent, heaven speaks. Here it announces the adventurous future and greatness for which the young rider on the white stallion is heading.

The Council began its sessions on April 9, 1488, in Ferrara. It was opened by Pope Eugene IV, who much preferred Ferrara to Basle, the city where the radical conciliarites had triumphed, passing the supremacy of the Council as dogma. As Eugene refused to recognize this, the Council deposed him as a heretic on June 25, 1439, and, on

November 5, it elected Duke Amadeus VIII of Savoy the new Pope. He took the name of Felix V and Enea Silvio de Piccolomini became his secretary at the Council. Amadeus is one of the really strange characters of history: the Emperor Sigismund elevated the Count of Savoy to the rank of Duke in 1416, thus making him the first Duke of his house, as the Council of Basle in 1439 made him the last anti-pope in Church history. There is a bronze statue of him in the chapel of the kings in Turin cathedral, where, as first Duke of Savoy, he and three successors mount guard over the shrine in which Christ's shroud was kept.

The woodcut by Tobias Stimmen is probably a better portrait of the *119* real Duke and Pope than this idealized statue put up by King Carl Albert in the nineteenth century. Tobias Stimmer, born in Schaffhausen in 1539, died in Strassburg in 1584 and is now regarded as one of Germany's most versatile masters of the late Renaissance. Of particular value are his portraits of the great, which he did as woodcuts for the books of his day. One of these is his portrait of Pope Felix V, which figures in the Basle chronicle. A rectangular frame composed of ornamental and imaginary figures surrounds an oval picture. Felix V is presented three-quarter face, wearing the vestment and tiara of the popes. In the top right hand is the coat of arms of Savoy, a white cross in a red field, surmounted by the tiara and the keys of Saint Peter. With Stimmer, the head is always the centre of a great wealth of ornamentation; dress, coat of arms, etc. and that of Felix V seems anything but a work of fantasy: in fact he has obviously been working from older portraits that were likenesses. The thoughtful face and well-shaped features beneath the tiara have aristocratic greatness and the dignity of the pious recluse, whose life he lived. This portrait confirms what the records of the Council suggest, namely that it was not only a rich, but also a good man that the rebellious Council Fathers elected as their anti-pope. He was crowned in the open air, in front of the tower side of Basle cathedral, which in those days had only just acquired the tower against which the statue of Saint George stands, this having been built *104* in 1414 by Ulrich von Einsingen, who also built the tower of Strassburg Minster. Crowned, the Pope went in solemn procession through the city. The streets were lined with cheering crowds. It was the climax of the Council.

The city was filled to overflowing with foreigners. The Council Fathers had all brought a suite of clerks and servants. Envoys and princes came and went, each with servants, musicians, quack-doctors and jugglers in their train. Basle had become an important place. There were years indeed, when it housed within its walls more foreigners than citizens. "Accommodation is expensive and becoming more and more so. Money goes less and less far, and there is a shortage of foodstuffs. There is meat enough for only half the people here, and every day brings new arrivals, more princes and prelates," a monk from Cluny wrote to his abbot in 1434. The confusion extended even to the coinage: there were Venetian ducats, Hungarian and Rhenish guilders, to say nothing of Italian, French, English and Spanish coins in circulation. It was harvest time for coiners and forgers. The City Council did its utmost to maintain order, issuing any amount of orders and prohibitions. "Since the Sacred Council is meeting here for the great cause of Christendom, each of us ought to be the better-behaved and more serious in our conduct." So the people of Basle were forbidden to carry swords, long knives or cudgels. Card-playing and dicing were forbidden. Men and women were no longer allowed to bathe together at the public baths.

The city of Basle was a confined though lovely setting for the Council. It had been rebuilt after the earthquake of 1356 and seemed to have been "made out of one mould". "There is no building here to tell of the old days," wrote Enea Silvio de Piccolomini, who was particularly impressed by the roofs of the houses and churches, which were of tiles arranged in coloured patterns. The present roof of the minster is a copy of one of these medieval roofs. Schedel's *Weltchronik* of 1493 contains a woodcut that shows what the city looked like in those days. On the west bank of the Rhine you see Greater Basle piled up round the cathedral hill. The minster still dominates the whole and is visible far and wide. The left-hand tower is still without its steeple. The architect, Hans von Nussdorf, was in fact busy finishing this second tower in that year. To all intents and purposes none of the houses and gateways shown in this woodcut have survived. Only the Spalentor, finished shortly before 1400 is still standing. Through it passes the road from Alsace and many of the Council Fathers must have entered the city that way. The house zur Mücke, in which the conclave elected Amadeus of Savoy Pope, was replaced by a new building in 1545. This is a plain,

118

124
123

171

172

179

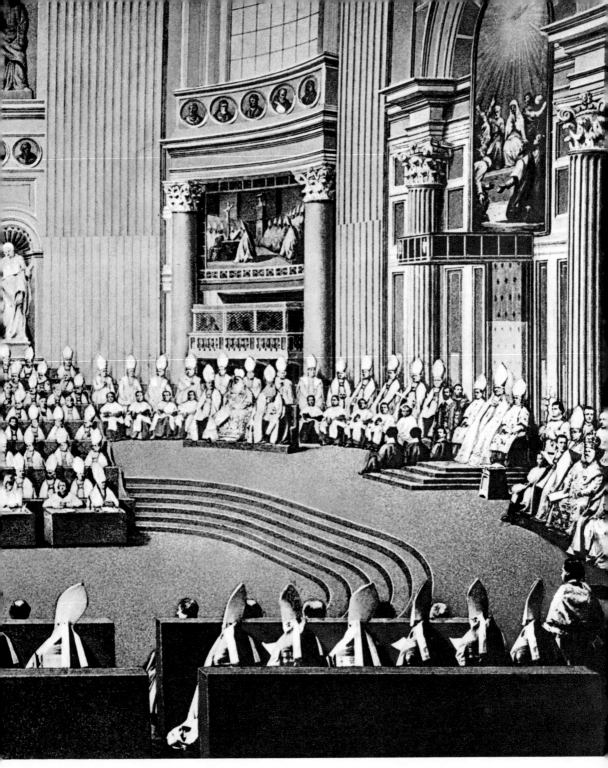

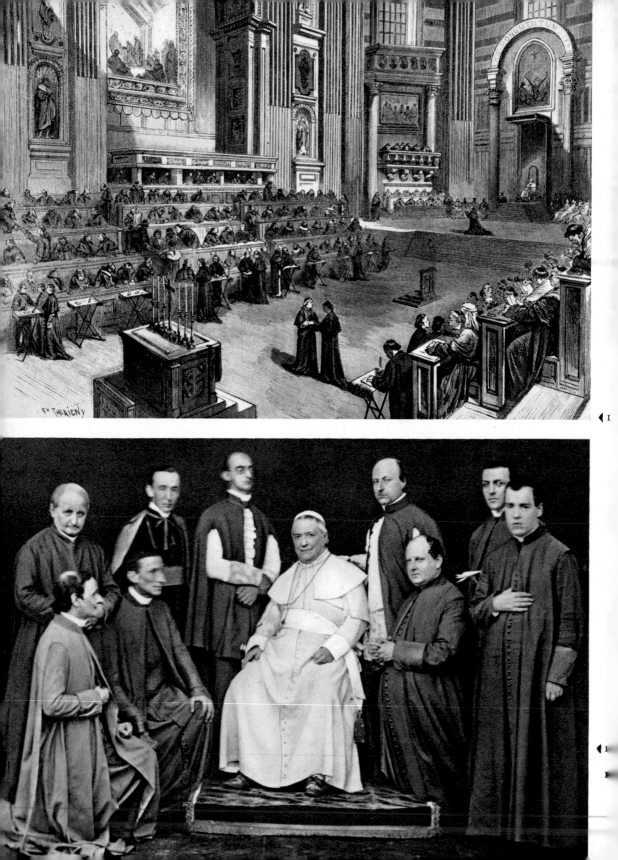

three-storeyed dwelling house with a high gabled roof, and largely corresponds to the guild house it replaced. We know that this is so from a marginal note made by Konrad Witz, the painter.

In the year 1434, the guild zum Himmel, which had painters, stone-masons, glass-painters and goldsmiths as its members, received into its company one, Master Konrad von Rothweil, whom today we call Konrad Witz. In 1435 he was made a burgher. Witz came to Basle because the Council was being held there, and the thought it the best place in which to find employment for his art. We know that about 1435 he painted the so-called Heilspiegel altar, though not for which church. Nine of its panels are now in Basle Museum of Art, two in Dijon Museum and one in the Berlin Museum. We can assume that this commission came his way because of the Council. We are more certain of the circumstances under which he painted a second masterpiece, the Peter altar in Geneva. In 1444, a prominent member of the Council, Bishop François de Mies, of Geneva, invited him to make a Peter altar for the cathedral of Saint Peter. The four panels that have survived carry the inscription HOC OPUS PINXIT CONRADUS SAPIENTIS DE BASILEA MCCCCIIII. In 1446 his wife is referred to as a widow, so that Witz's productive period coincides with that of the Council. The Council of Basle debated questions concerning art and took no decision that affected religious or other painting, but it certainly provided scope for the greatest Swiss painter of the early Renaissance.

Witz presents the saints as though they were burgesses of Basle. He has given them the faces of the craftsmen of his guild and so exact is his detail, that you are sure you could feel the softness of the fur and the rough surface of the linen, if you just touched them with your fingertips. Men and women stand with feet firmly planted and the background extends behind them, impressive and exact. The interior remind you of Basle Minster. The events depicted in the *Heilspiegelaltar* are being enacted before the golden ground that in all medieval painting represented the infinite space of heaven. In the picture depicting the draught *121, 122* of fishes, one of the great panels of the Geneva Peter altar that has been preserved, Christ's head has as its background a littoral landscape that is still identifiable by its detail as part of the shore of Lake Geneva. Nicolas von Cues and the humanists discovered Nature via Science. Conrad Witz was the first German painter to accord it the honour of inclusion in an altar-piece. Here the events of the bible are taking place in a landscape familiar to the beholder. The saints are contemporaries, and the places in which they are presented are the churches or streets of Geneva and Basle. In one of his later works, depicting Saint Catharine *120* and Saint Magdalene, now in Strassburg, one of the saints is shown in a late Gothic transept, which looks onto a burgess's dwelling house, a narrow, high-gabled building of two storeys. The structure looks *123* familiar, and it is, in fact, the Guild House zur Mücke in Basle.

The Basle Council was a gathering of the fifteenth-century men who changed the face of the world. We do not know whether Witz met Nicolas von Cues, Enea Silvio de Piccolomini and Giuliano de Cesarini; but as a painter, he was an artisan and thus in a different class, so he probably did not. Historically, of course, he belongs to their circle, for he has achieved in paint, what they did in words and thought.

The Council Fathers in Basle assured the churchmen of Byzantium that it was quite possible for an elderly prelate to travel in his bed all the way from Constantinople to the landing places in Basle; but the Byzantines were not to be enticed and they went to Ferrara in answer to the Pope's call. Thus, when Eugene IV opened the new session of the Council on April 9, 1438, he had sitting at his feet in Ferrara cathedral the Emperor John VIII, Palaeologus, Patriarch Joseph of Constantinople, Archbishop Bessarion of Nicaea, Archbishop Isidor of Kiev and the legates of the patriarchs of Antioch, Jerusalem and Alexandria. This was the greatest day in the city's history, yet Ferrara seems to have forgotten it. Today, the city's buildings are plastered with inscriptions proudly recording this or that event, but nowhere is there any mention of the Council. If you are determined to track it down, you will find in the Cathedral Museum a disregarded relief of a man's bearded head. Beneath this is the inscription: "Bessario Cardinalio qui in proxismis aedibus Sa Maria Hypates habitavit quo tempore Ferriae Concilium habitatum." (In memory of Cardinal Bessarion, who stayed in the houses beside Sa Maria Hypates while attending the Council of Ferrara). These houses were destroyed either in the earthquake of the sixteenth century or in the air raids of the twentieth century. Ferrara has nothing more to tell us of Johannes Bessarion, Archbishop of Nicaea, the Council town of Asia Minor, whom Eugene IV made a cardinal, but it was in his Roman house that the Humanists of the West met and without him and his library, which was to form the nucleus of the library of Saint Mark's in Venice, we should not have known much about Plato. He became Latin patriarch of Constantinople ten years after the end of the Byzantine Empire and died in Ravenna in 1472. He *127* was buried in the Roman basilica of Santa Apostoli, of which he was cardinal, and its Franciscans put up a memorial to him there in 1682. This is let into one of the pillars of the church and consists of an inscription praising his deeds and virtues and a medallion with a bust of him in high relief: the bearded face of an Eastern sage beneath the hat of a Roman cardinal.

Ferrara Cathedral stands in the very heart of the city like a gigantic reliquary. Ranks of dwarf galleries comprised of fantastic little pillars *126* under semicircular arches occupy its south side, on which, at ground floor, a peculiar structure has been built, the so-called shopkeepers' loggia. A long arcade takes one past a row of tiny shops, and in the upper storey are tiny dwelling-and store-rooms for the shopkeepers. This strange flight of architectural and commercial fancy ends in the four-storeyed tower designed by L. B. Alberti, one of the fathers of Italian Renaissance architecture, and built about 1412.

The cathedral is one of the great buildings of Lombardy. Designed in richly ornamented style of Italian Romanesque, it was begun in 1135 and completed about 1300 in the period of transition between the rounded and the pointed arch, the façade completing what the southern *125* side hints at. The lower part is plain and simple, but then come three storeys of fantastic colonnades and windows, so that you scarcely see the wall behind, this being veiled by pillars, windows and arches of the finest chisel-work. This dream in stone reaches its height in the central portal, whose fantastically shaped pillars are carried by lions that also have sphinxes on their backs. Above, the arch of the portal supports an open balcony with pillars. In the centre, dominating this, is the Madonna carved by Christoforo da Firenze in 1427. The gable space is occupied by apocalyptic carvings of the Last Judgment.

We can imagine this dream of saints and traders transformed into stone encouraging the longings of those who wished to reunite the Faith in East and West. Visiting the cathedral now, you no longer see it as it was when the Council met there, for the interior was reconstructed in 1711. A drawing made in that year shows a plain romanic-Gothic

interior that, as in the Italian way, seems far simpler than its ornamented exterior. Nor can we imagine what the city of Ferrara itself
looked like in those days. Opposite the cathedral there is still the
d'Estes' first castle. They were the Pope's deputies there, and later the
reigning princes of Ferrara. A few hundred yards farther on stands the
128   mighty, four-towered fort in which Pope Eugene IV stayed during the
Council. The stout red brick walls of the water-fort have been a little
softened by the ornamentation of later years, when Italy's great poets,
Tasso and Ariosto, lived at the court in Ferrara.

In the fifteenth century, Ferrara was a city of commerce, though
it could not compete with the financial power of Florence. Pope Eugene
IV had undertaken to provide for the seven hundred Byzantine Council
Fathers and legates while they were attending the Council, but this was
asking too much of his finances and before long he was glad to accept an
offer of help from notoriety-hunting Florentines, whose pockets were
better lined than his, and on January 16, 1439, he transferred the
129–131   Council to Florence. As Brunelleschi had only recently completed the
cupola for the cathedral there, the sight of that and of the baptistery
must have made the Byzantines feel very much at home. The walls of
the baptistery, which are inlaid with white and green marble, are
reminiscent of architecture on the Bosporus, which tries both to veil
space and to extend it into infinity, instead of restricting it with walls;
yet at the same time they make the interior seem even more severe.
Bernhard von Clairvaux once said in a tirade against the Gothic cathedral, "in God's house I want neither exaggerated height, immeasurable
length, yawning width, lavish ornamentation nor remarkable paintings,
because all those are things that attract the gaze of people at their
prayers and hinder them in the true love of God," and the people of
Florence seem to have accepted this view when building their cathedral
centuries later. Florence cathedral, designed by Arnolfo di Cambio in
1296, and in all essentials finished by Giovanni Ghinia and Orcanga
after 1360, was to have a clear, plain interior, strictly ordered and down
to earth. Arnolfo di Cambio did use the multiple pillar and pointed
arch of Gothic, but what he built with them was no heavenward striving
dream structure, but a firmly anchored heavy hall, and it was in this
that the Council Fathers from East and West reached agreement.

Since the day of Charlemagne, the Church of the East had disputed the addition to the Creed of *filioque*, which meant that the Holy Ghost proceeded from the Father *and* the Son, but now the Byzantines agreed to accept this, and, what is more, they also accepted the dogma of the primacy of the Pope. The so-called Union bull, the original of which we still have, puts it thus: "The apostolic throne and the Pope possess primacy over the entire globe; the Pope, as Peter's successor and Christ's deputy, is head of the entire Church, Father and teacher of all Christians, and has the authority to govern the entire Church in conformity with the acts and canons of the old councils." It was drawn up in both Latin and Greek, and was read out at the session of July 6, 1439, the Latin version by Cardinal Giuliano de Cesarini, the Greek by Archbishop Bessarion.

The story of this as told in stone by the Florentine sculptor, Filarete, *132–134* is as objective and precise as the interior of Florence cathedral. You can still see it on the portal of Saint Peter's in Rome, where, as we already know, the coronation of King Sigismund is depicted. In this second series of sculptured pictures you see the Greeks taking ship in Constantinople, then going ashore in an Italian port. You see the envoy of the patriarch entering Rome and paying homage to the Pope; you see Cardinal Cesarini and Archbishop Bessarion reading out the Union bull in the cathedral at Florence, while Emperor and Pope listen; finally you see the Greeks boarding ships to a fanfare of trumpets on their way home. Filarete has not even forgotten the union with the Armenians concluded on November 22. He depicts their patriarch receiving the bull from the hands of Eugene himself, and how he has delighted in their oriental vestments, their hats and beards, at the same time as emphasizing what is the essence of the whole event. His heads look as though they were likenesses. We learn from him, too, that the Byzantine ships had thwarts and sails, and also the state in which the walls of Rome were in the year 1439.

In the 1480's people liked sculpture that was as close to Nature as Filarete's plastic reportage, and Italy's greatest genius of the arts, Leonardo da Vinci, said, "Painting is a true daughter of Nature, or rather her granddaughter. Because all created things have been produced by Nature, and from them comes the art of painting." Yet Cosimo de Medici, the banker, "Father of his Fatherland" and uncrowned king of Florence, seems not to have thought much of Leonardo's con-

136 cept of closeness to Nature in art; for, when looking for a painter to do the murals in the chapel of the Palazzo Medici-Riccardi, he chose Benozzo Gozzoli from nearby Pistoia. Gozzoli was a pupil of the angelic painter-monk, Fra Angelico. Painting, he composed legends in colour, and the subject Cosimo commissioned him to paint was well suited to such treatment. It was the story of the Three Kings, and you see these noble horsemen wearing gorgeous garments and with oriental crowns on their heads, riding through forest and meadows, while ardent men and lovely women make up their retinues. Nature blooms as though on the first day of creation.

Although the chapel lies along an outside wall it has no window, so that the murals did not become visible till the candles were lit. Then the crowns and haloes glittered like gold against the green of the woods; the kings' coats were of brocades such as no one has yet seen, and the cavalcade stretched on and on into a landscape to which there is no end.

Giorgio Vasari, the first art historian, accused Benozzo Gozzoli of being a reactionary Gothic dreamer, and later critics followed his example, until it was discovered that several Medicis appear among the men and women in the kings' retinues, faithfully portrayed. It was still more surprising to find that the king riding alone with a small suite is *135* none other than John VIII Palaeologus, Emperor of Constantinople, his handsome face clouded with melancholy. He is gazing up at his star, scrutinizing and somewhat doubtful. Where the Emperor is, the *137* Patriarch Joseph cannot be far away, and indeed there he is riding out from behind the rim of the picture, a fantastic crown on his head, his face speaking of both power and intelligence. You can see that this bearded man of God knew the rules and art of diplomacy and in no way despised life. The Byzantines had their own terms for worldly clerics of this kind; they called them "politicians".

John Palaeologus died in 1448, eleven years before the murals in the Medici Chapel were painted. After that great day in Florence, the West speedily forgot all about him and his empire and no one lifted a finger to help his successor, when the Turks, under Mehmed the Conqueror, launched the final assault on Constantinople in 1453, that cost him both his life and empire. One painter, however, had obviously not forgotten the handsome Emperor, whom he had seen at the Council in Florence and made him one of the Three Kings.

The crowning of Felix V in front of Basle Minster and the union with the Greek Church proclaimed in Florence cathedral were the antithecal climaxes of the Basle Council. After these triumphs, Council and anti-Council became bogged down. Felix V transferred the remains of the Basle Council to his residence, Lausanne, and Eugene IV transferred his legitimate Council from Florence to Rome. Unfortunately, the results achieved at Florence and Basle and which the world applauded, did not endure. The union with the Greek Church was wrecked by the opposition of the Byzantine clergy, and Emperor John's hopes of getting the West to help him against the Turks came to nothing. Felix V saw his supporters deserting him one by one, and when Enea Silvio de Piccolomini, now Council secretary of Emperor Frederick III, a son-in-law of Emperor Sigismund, rebelled against him and won the Emperor for Rome, the Empire turned against him too. It made its own agreement with Eugene IV's successor, Pope Nicholas V, in the Vienna Concordat of February 17, 1448. On April 7, 1449, the Duke of Savoy, drew the logical conclusions. Pope Felix V retired. Thanks to the vision of a nobleman, the last schism of the Church ended in the agreement, which the best men of the Basle Council had sought to bring about.

TRENT–BOLOGNA

"THEREFORE, where necessity requires it and the Pope causes offence to Christendom, who ever can do so, must, as true member of the corporate body, see that there is a truly free Council, and who can do this better than the secular sword," thus Martin Luther in his book addressed "to the Christian Nobles of the German Nation," which was published in 1520. It was on October 31, 1517, eight months after the Fifth Council in the Lateran, that he nailed his ninety-five theses to the door of the church in Wittenberg. Three years later, at the Reichstag in Wurms, at which Luther's teachings were discussed, there were cries of "Council, Council!" But Luther, who in Augsburg in 1518 had called for "a better informed Pope and a general Council," did not think quite as much of the Council as his book led people to believe. In 1519, during his famous disputation with Johannes Eck, he said that even a general Council could err. Where he was concerned, the final instance was Holy Writ. The Popes of the day, Leo X (1513–1521), Hadrian VI (1522–1523) and Clement VII (1523–1524) shunned the Council for different reasons. The Pope's experiences of the Councils of Basle and Constance had not made them favourably inclined towards the Council as an institution, and had left them afraid that the conciliar theory might triumph, if a new one were held. The Reichstag at Nürnberg had called for a "general, free, Christian Council in German lands," following Luther's idea, and the struggle between the Emperor and the King of France for the leadership in Europe made such a thing even more desirable. As it happened, it was not till a generation after Luther's emergence that the Great Third Reform Council was held. Pope Paul III (1534–1549) convened it for May 22, 1542, an earlier attempt to hold an Ecumenical Council in Mantua and Vicenza in 1537 having been frustrated by the confusions of war. The hazards of war also delayed the new Council, for it was December 13, 1545 before the papal

185

186

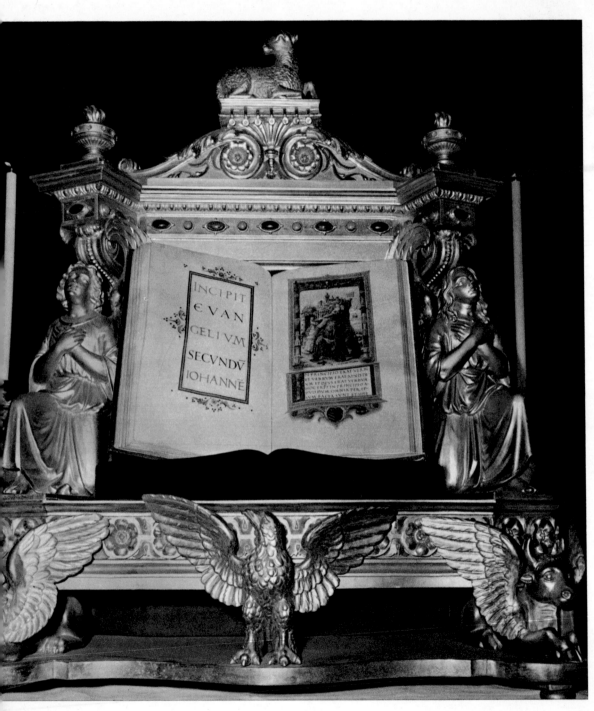

189

legate, Cardinal del Monte, opened it, the Nineteenth General Council, in the cathedral of Trent.

Trent is one of the cities that has cherished the memory of the Council held in it. The houses and palaces, which the Council Fathers used have marble plaques on which are their names and the words "Citta del Concilio". The Council churches, that is the Cathedral and Santa Maria Maggiore, are the same inside as when the Council met in them. The crossings in which the Fathers assembled, still have the seats of honour in them. Both churches possess paintings depicting sessions of the Council. The city of Trent is still aware that in the years 1545–1563, it was the centre of Christendom and the focus of its hopes of a uniform faith.

Trent was a bishop's see in the fourth century A.D. and then, in 1004, the dominion of its bishop was replaced by that of the dukes of Lombardy. The cathedral of Saint Vigilius, dedicated to the first bishop of Trent, stands on foundations dating back to the fourth century. Prince Federico Vanga, its bishop from 1207–1217, began rebuilding it. Its first architect is supposed to be Adamo d'Arogno, who has put his name on one of the stones of the apse. His sons and grandsons continued building it, and it was not finished till 1309. In 1400 it was vaulted. The tower was completed during the fifteenth century, the cupola being erected over the crossing in 1520.

The Lombardic rounded arch has made a masterpiece of Trent *138–140* cathedral. Its architects came from its home, Como. The walls are of free stone. Under the eaves of the roof is a line of arches. Twin pillars coupled at their feet and at their capitals, although slender and delicate, together have the strength to carry the massive rounded arches. Between them and the wall is an open gallery. Higher up, the octagonal tower over the crossing repeats this pattern, having a diadem-like arcade under its roof, as have the half-towers on its four flanks. On ground level, it is only the apse of the choir and the housings of the doorways that are decorated with pillars and animal effigies. The lovely canopy of the east door, which is late thirteenth century and so approaching the pointed arch of Gothic, rests its pillars on the patient backs of lions, which the Allrighteous honours as his heraldic animal. The interior is a three-aisled basilica. Stout multiple-shafted pillars separate the broad nave *140* from the side aisles. The round-arched windows have never been enlarged, and to our eyes, spoiled where light is concerned, they seem small and the interior unusually gloomy; but in that respect it is as it originally was. The transept has extra light from the crossing, and the choir too is better lit.

The Council worked on three levels, as it were. In the congregation of theologians, learned theologians propounded their views of the questions up for discussion. All discussion was in general congregation, and decisions reached there were voted on in the solemn sessions of the Council itself, which were held in the cathedral. There is a painting in the Louvre depicting one of these sessions. It is considered to be the work of one of the greatest painters of the sixteenth century, Tiziano Vecellio (1476–1576), usually known as Titian. It shows the Council *141* Fathers gathered in two groups in the nave, wearing the white mitres mentioned in connection with the opening of the Vienne Council. In the foreground are their attendants and the guard of honour. The scene is framed by the mighty pillars of the nave, against which are the multi-gabled canopies of altars. Everyone's attention is turned on a group of four cardinals sitting in front of the altar, with secretaries squatting at their feet. To the right and left of the cardinals are other Council Fathers seated in the choir stalls. The altar rises up in front of the high wall of the rood-loft. The mitres gleam whitely above the purple and red of the vestments, while the polished grey of the steel armour and helmets vies with the grey of the stone of the pillars. In the shadows, the colours break and merge into a background like in the waters of the lagoon in Venice. You can scarcely distinguish figures and gestures. The painter has presented the incident as a whole: the ceremonial atmosphere, the majesty of the moment and the liturgical accomplishment are all there. The occasion has found a painter worthy of it, whether he really was Titian or another Venetian. In the painting, there is a cross above the altar, on which Christ hangs crucified, head turned to the left in his mortal torment. It is not difficult to identify this as the one now in the *142* Chapel of the Cross, in which surroundings of baroque statuary it appears medieval, which it indeed is, most probably a product of the early fifteenth century. The head of the Christ is full of the cruel pain of the mystic, while his body and loin-cloth display the physical joy and faithful observation of nature of the Renaissance. Today, the crucifix stands between statues of Mary and Saint John the Evangelist, both contemporary works, though not of the same artist. These were not there in Titian's day. In his picture of the Council the crucifix stands up alone above the altar.

The other painter seems to have made a more accurate painting, for he puts the Council Fathers not in rows one behind the other, but arranged in a long oval that fills the nave. The leading Council Fathers have each a Latin numeral, and the key with their names is underneath. There are small altar-canopies against the pillars, on which armorial shields also hang, high up. To the east, an altar closes the oval and on it is the crucifixion group such as it is today in the Chapel of the Cross.

148

This picture, darkened by the candle-soot and dust of centuries, now hangs in the choir, Apparently. even at its best, it had none of the magic and greatness of the Louvre painting. "That makes its painter more accurate. He has produced a document; while Titian, like all geniuses, used his imagination." That is what the beholder thinks at first glance and becomes jealous and suspicious as soon as he sees the second picture of the Council by this unknown artist in the cathedral. In arrangement it corresponds to the first, but shows fewer people. Here, in fact, the artist has painted one of the sessions of the general congregation, held in Santa Maria Maggiore, erroneously depicting it as being in the cathedral. Someone who deals so unscrupulously with historical fact, could also have made a mistake about the crucifix. The error becomes understandable, when you remember that these two paintings are later votive pictures, presented in memory of the Council in 1703, when the crypt still lay under the high choir, as you see it in the background. It was demolished in 1739. "Ex voto ob liberationem huius civitatis ursidione gallorum et coniuratorum secutam, 8 febris 1703", said the inscription on the picture. "Promised and presented as a thanksoffering for the liberation of this city from the oppression of Gauls and conspirators on February 8, 1703." The Gauls and conspirators are the French and Bavarians, who had invaded Tirol in 1703 during the war of the Spanish succession.

The choice of meeting place for the Council was influenced by the wish to protect the synod from the hazards of the wars that filled the sixteenth century, and in this it was successful. None the less, the strife in the world was a threat to the Council, and therefore, before each session, the Council Fathers were given a symbolical, palpable reminder of the

Peace of God in which their deliberations ought to be conducted. A priest held out the strumentum Pacis for them to kiss. This is preserved among the cathedral's treasures. Base, pillars, columns, entablature and a gable with cross and urn provide the frame for the centre-piece, a

143 golden plaque, which has the Lamb of God engraved on it and, below it, the date, 1534. The base has engraved on it the word UNITAS in Roman capitals and a bundle of rods as an exhortation to unity. Since the thirteenth century priests had held these pax-boards for communicants to kiss before communion, and no doubt one of those used in Trent cathedral was selected for this use during the Council, and perhaps expressly furnished with the inscription on its basis because of that.

The general Congregation had its session at first in Palazzo Prato, the seat of the papal legate, then in the church of Santa Maria Maggiore, a more modern building than the thirteenth century cathedral. Cardinal

145, 146 Prince Bernard Cles, Bishop of Trent, had it built in 1520–1523 by Antonio Medaglia, who, like the architect who built the cathedral, came from Como. Medaglia, who had learned under Bramante, furnished the outer walls with a line of stout half-pillars. The entrance side is dominated by a figure Renaissance portal, above which is a romanesque rosette. There are romanesque elements too in the belfry that rises from the left-hand outer wall. The exterior with its raised centre part leads one to expect an interior like a basilica, but instead there is an extensive hall with chapels of ease off either side. Between these are double pillars, and a massive barrel-vault roofs the great nave. Slim windows admit more light to the choir, which also has a painted roof by Romamino or l'Albini depicting the Triumph of Our Lady. The sessions of the Council held in this late Renaissance setting are the subject of a painting that now hangs on the left wall of the crossing and

147 is attributed to Francesco Naurizio. It depicts the twenty-second session either of the Congregation of Theologians or of the general congregation, at which the nature and meaning of holy Mass was discussed. A learned Jesuit, Laynez, is in the pulpit in the background giving his views. In the middle is the Council's secretary, Angelo Massarelli seated at a table, in front of which a crucifix has been planted, taking down the minutes. In front of the table is the speaker's seat of honour, occupied by King Philip II of Spain. Round these two poles the Council Fathers are seated in a semicircle facing the papal legate and more important cardinals, who, as usual, have their secretaries squatting at their feet. This session is being held in the nave of Santa Maria Maggiore. There is a second painting of this session which agrees with the other in most of the detail, except that the pulpit is occupied not by Laynez, the Jesuit, but by a bearded figure wearing a white mitre. This is the painting which the Venetian engravers, the leading picture-reporters of sixteenth-century Europe, took as the picture of the Council, simplified and published in a great number of copies. For generations people's idea of a Council was based on this picture.

Like the cathedral, Santa Maria Maggiore has preserved its Council crucifix, a wooden one not unlike that of the cathedral. Today, it stands on the altar of the Epiphany Chapel. The church still treasures the Strumentum Pacis. Like that of the cathedral, the Pax-board has an *144* architectural frame, though a plainer one, but its centre-piece is more sumptuous, showing in high relief suffering Christ being supported by two angels between the knees of his lamenting mother.

Cardinal Count Mark Sittich von Altemps, also known as Count Hohenems, cut a bad figure as papal legate at the Council of Trent, thus, although Pope Pius IV's nephew, he soon vanished from the College of Legates, which began its third convention in 1562. Cardinals who did not even know Latin had no business at Trent. In 1569, Altemps commissioned Onorio Longhi to build him a family chapel in the Roman basilica of Santa Maria in Trastavere. Pasquale Cati da Jesi, later an admirer of Michaelangelo and Raphael painted its murals and Cardinal Altemps took the opportunity to ensure that his participation in the Council of Trent should be duly recorded for posterity, having *150* Cati da Jesi paint a session of the Council. As he had not attended one himself, Cati da Jesi worked from one of these Venetian engravings of 1565, simplifying it further to suit his own purposes. In his version, the line of seats opposite the open semicircle is occupied only by the papal legates, one of whom is recognizably Cardinal Altemps. On the wall behind the cardinal hang the armorial bearings of his uncle, Pius IV. Cati da Jesi could use the Venetian engraving with a good conscience, for the painting on which it was based did in fact depict a session of 1562 in which Altemps had taken part as one of the papal legates. He has merely altered its shape, compressing it and making it taller, so as to give himself a large foreground to fill with the associated ideas required by Mannerism that was the fashion in his day. Rather strangely, he has depicted the Church as a young woman, who not only holds the double-cross of the patriarchs in her hand, but has put a papal tiara on her curly head. She is triumphant. Earth and the books of learning lie at her feet. The world, in the guise of various female allegorical figures, does her homage: among the figures is, on the left, the city of Rome, wearing a helmet and energetically clasping a lictor's fasces and axe, the symbol of authority in ancient Rome. This fashion of Mannerism flourished between 1520 and 1600, it was always striving to amaze and entertain the beholder. One of its peculiar principles was to conceal the main subject behind an incidental one, which was placed prominently in the foreground, the object being to make the whole more interesting.

149   A little way in from the main door of the church of Santa Maria in Aracoeli on the Capitol in Rome, is the impressive seated figure of Pope Paul III set on a high pedestal. He makes a majestic figure as he sits there on his throne, the arm-rests of which end in lion's heads, right hand raised didactically—or is it threateningly? The face under the tiara and framed by well-trimmed full beard, appears hard, perhaps even grand, but at any rate resolute. The folds of the robes are crisp and the cloak is like a great tent round the broad shoulders. This is Alessandro Farnese, from 1534 to 1549 Pope Paul III, but before that father of Pier-Luigi and of Constanza Farnese, and thus founder of one of the most important princely families of Italy. Whoever made this statue was a master of portraiture, for no one else has depicted Paul III so truly as the unobjectionable Renaissance prince he was.

151   No other Pope has had as many portraits made as Paul III. In one famous painting of him he is shown as a delicate, almost fragile old man sitting in his room. To the left and behind him stand a bearded cardinal, while from the right some person of rank is approaching, almost stealthily, the Pope watching him mistrustfully, like an old fox. The three are Paul III, his grandson, Cardinal Alessandro Farnese, and Prince Ottavio who later became Duke of Parma and son-in-law of Emperor Charles V. This portrait of Pope Paul III is by Titian and one of the greatest paintings of the century. "In the year 1545 he was summoned to Rome by Cardinal Farnese. There he found Vasari, who had returned from Naples, and was painting the hall of the Cancelleria for the cardinal. Farnese recommended Titian to Vasari, and the latter took great pleasure in his company and showed him the sights of Rome. After a few days rest, Titian was given accommodation in Belvedere and commissioned to make another portrait of Pope Paul, Farnese and Duke Ottavio, all in full figure. This he did most admirably to the great satisfaction of his subjects." Thus Giorgio Vasari, painter and first of the art historians, proud of having met the painter-prince from Venice.

Titian knew the Pope, who had sat for him in Bologna in 1543. (The resulting portrait now hangs in the National Museum in Naples.) What the ambitious, art-minded cardinal now wanted was a group showing him and his brother with the Pope, that would equal, if not surpass the one Raphael had painted of Leo X and his nephews. Titian saw through *56* his subjects and read the secrets of their hearts. This group is a tense uncanny revelation of the secret tension, flattery, calculation and dastardly falseness in the Farnese family, that so often clouded the relations of the Pope and his grandsons. Here is a weak old man, gorgeously robed by Titian in white and red, looking towards Ottavio with an expression of strained attention and a smile in which is love, but behind it, also the mistrust of bitter experience.

Pope Paul III was one of those who could have said to their critics with André Gide: "Please don't understand me too quickly." He was a harmless, gay Renaissance prince, but also more, much more. In his complicated disputes and negotiations with Emperor Charles V and Francis I of France, with the Italian cities and princes, and not least with his own son and, latterly, his unreliable grandson, Paul proved himself the master diplomat of his century. He knew people, but loved them none the less.

It would have been surprising had there been no other statue of this great man, but there is: another statue that shows yet another side of him. In the Pope's own church, that of Saint Peter's in Rome, his tomb stands in a privileged place, to the left of the Cattedra Petri. It was made in 1552, the work of Guglielmo della Porta, and began a new *152* trend in monuments to the dead: depicting the live person rather than the corpse. Sarcophagus and base together form a hill, on top of which Paul III sits like Moses on Sinai. At his feet are the marble effigies of Justice and Prudence, depicted, as was the way then, as female figures. Justitia is young and holds the lictor's fasces playfully on her arm. The model must have been a physically lovely woman in her prime, and the quick-witted Romans pronounced her Paul III's voluptuous sister, Julia Farnese, who was regarded as the mistress of the Borgia Pope, Alexander VI. Were these evil tongues silenced, when the marble statue was encased in an unfortunate garb of tin?

Paul III triumphed over the legacy of his youth, over rumour and error. This bowed, but beautiful old man wears neither the tiara nor any other headgear. The bearded face has the features both of the Renaissance prince of Santa Maria in Aracoeli and of the aged diplomat of Titian's group, merged into a third, more exalted version. Here we have Paul III the humanist, the Pope of the Council of Trent, who spent most of his life striving for the unity of Christendom. We can believe that this man made John Fisher, whom Henry VIII had beheaded, a cardinal, that he twice demanded that the Conquistadors allow the South American Indians their rights as human beings instead of persecuting them. This, too, is the Pope whom Rome has to thank for such buildings of enduring beauty as the Capitol square and the Palazzo Farnese. He gave Michaelangelo the commission for the Last Judgment in the Sistine Chapel, and in 1547, put him in charge of building Saint Peter's.

The contradictions and contrasts in the character of Paul III were reflected in the personalities of his legates to the Council. The most senior was Cardinal Giovanni Maria Ciocchi del Monte. An incident that took place on July 30, 1546, shows what sort of a person he was. The troops of the Schmalkaldic League of Protestant Princes were threatening the passes across the Alps and Del Monte wanted to transfer the Council to a safer place. When his proposal encountered opposition, he became so aggressive that Cardinal Paccheco, a Spaniard, called out: "You are treating the Council Fathers like servants," and Cardinal Madruzzo, Prince Bishop of Trent, told Del Monte to his face that his behaviour was not that of a noble. And, actually noble is what Del Monte was not, as one can see from Scipione Pulzone's portrait of him. For this he chose the form of the medallion. Del Monte looks at us out of its oval frame, his eyes boding no good, the nose ordinary, the full beard unable to conceal the coldness of the mouth. Pulzone depicts him in the Pope's house garb, for when this was painted, Cardinal Del Monte was already Pope Julius III (1550–1555), though this high office had certainly not made him any less of a libertine: bull fighting, hunting and carnival were his favourite occupations. He had his "favourites", one of whom he made a cardinal at the age of seventeen! Julius III was a Roman, but he did not like Romans. It is no wonder that the only things that keep his memory alive today are the Villa Giulia, which now houses the Etruscan Museum, and Palzone's portrait of him in the Galleria Spada.

It is all very different with the second papal legate, Cardinal Marcello Cervini. The Florentine painter, Francesco Salviati, painted him during the Council of Trent, probably in 1548. This portrait is today *153* one of the treasures of the Galleria Borghese in Rome. The cardinal is shown in a panelled room. On the right-hand wall are the half-pillars and gable of the Renaissance, and in the background are two doors. Cervini is sitting in an armchair at a table, on which lies a costly rug, richly coloured and with a meticulously worked pattern. On this lies an open book, and beside it stands a hand-bell. The cardinal is holding the book in his slim hands. He has obviously just looked up from reading it and is still in its world, his gaze turned inward, not at the beholder. As a young man, Cervini studied astronomy, mathematics, architecture and archaeology at Vienna. He wrote a report on calendar reform for Clement VII and, in 1543, was made one of the papal legates to the Council of Trent. He was the opposite of the coarse, unbridled Del Monte: a pious, dedicated priest, who continually thought of practical reforms and righteousness. He was elected Pope on April 9, 1555 and chose the name of Marcellus II, but died on May 1 of that same year. On the occasion of his death the humanist, Onofrio Panvini, said with Virgil: "Fate did not wish to show him to us." Francesco Salviati's portrait does this great cardinal and Pope justice, both in its depiction of his character and the fineness of its colouring. His use of that dangerous colour pink with red is masterly. Here everything is subordinated to the face: the forehead is high, the mouth hidden by a full beard, but the eyes! They look at you without seeing you. They are directed at a world where thought is free.

The Emperor Charles V made Cardinal Cervini responsible for drawing up the plans for transferring the Council to some place in Italy; however, there was soon no longer any need for the Council to leave Trent, as the Emperor had managed to repulse the advancing

Protestant troops. The Council was then able to resume its discussion of justification which it had begun in July. This was one of the all-important questions and Cervini took a prominent part in drawing up the decree comprising the Council's decisions. This received the approval of the assembled Council at its sixth session of January 7, 1547. By justification is understood things done by which God makes it possible for sinful man to attain to heaven. Luther believed that justification of sinners before God could only be accomplished through faith in Christ's act of redemption. The Council of Trent, however, insisted that people's will must also be involved and give the divine grace active help. Thus man can acquire merit that will help towards his redemption. Luther insisted that the man justified before God remained in the last resort a sinner. Justification merely covered up his sin. The Council of Trent took the view that Grace effected an inner hallowing, through which man's sins were cancelled, and its decree speaks of Sanctifying Grace.

The viewpoints of the Council of Trent and the Reformation are not contradictory, as might appear. Both are based on the old, old discussion of man's justification before God that reaches far back into Church history, and that is why certain historians consider that the schism of the Reformation would have been avoided, if this doctrine of justification had been promulgated at the Fifth Lateran Council in 1512–1517.

Martin Luther was now dead. He died in the second year of the Council, February 18, 1546, in Eisleben, where he was born. Lucas Cranach the Elder and his son Lucas painted various portraits of him. In fact, the elder Cranach, court painter at Wittenberg, was his personal friend. His best portraits are those he did in that period of his creativity, when his work was full of drama. The round portrait, now in Basle, was done at this time. Luther has a big fleshy face, in which soul and spirit strive for expression. Cranach's colouring and modelling is as strong as the language in which Luther wrote his translation of the Bible. Cranach shows the passionate reformer, the man who believed the end of the world was approaching, the popular preacher who carried his audience away, the early Christian theologian.

On March 6, 1547, Bishop von Capaccio died in Trent, and the next day several other Council Fathers also died. The Council doctor,

Fracastoro, a specialist in infectious diseases, diagnosed spotted fever. Cardinal Madruzzo, who had been able to persuade the Council to remain in Trent though the Protestant troops were approaching the Alpine passes, had to capitulate once this new enemy was discovered within the city's walls. At the session of March 11, 1547 a majority vote decided to transfer the seat of the Council to Bologna. The minority of fourteen bishops took the view that it should remain in Trent, because its transference elsewhere might mean "the return of the German who persisted in the error of his way and thus endangers the peace and unity of the Church." The leader of this minority was Cardinal Christoforo Madruzzo (1512–1572), of Schloss Madruzzo in the valley of the Arca. His father had been Ferdinand I's imperial councillor and commandant of the militia of the bishopric of Trent during the Peasant's War. Christoforo had studied in Padua, Bologna and Paris. He was made Bishop of Trent on August 1, 1539, and on November 28, 1543 Pope Paul III made him a cardinal. All his life Madruzzo remained faithful to the Emperor and advocated his interests at the Reichstags of Nürnberg, Wurms and, especially, at the Council of Trent.

In his biography of Titian, Vasari writes: "In the year 1541, he painted a portrait of Don Diego di Mendoza, then ambassador of Emperor Charles V to Venice. He is depicted standing, full length, a fine figure of a man. From then on Titian began painting some portraits full length and this became the custom. This was the way in which he painted the Cardinal of Trent when the latter was still young." Here he *156* means Cardinal Christoforo Madruzzo and the portrait in question was painted in February and March of 1542. It is today one of the treasures of the Metropolitan Museum in New York. The young Bishop of Trent is shown standing in front of a brocade curtain, left hand resting lightly on a table. As always with Titian, the subject is very much the thing and the figure of the young man fills the picture. His bishop's garb seems fitting and proper. The oval, finely chiselled face possesses a well-balanced combination of strength and spirit. The small beard frames a strong jaw. The eyes are pensive and unseeing. That this is a good likeness is confirmed by the heads of him on coins and the engraving of him published after his death. In these the heaviness of build, such as you find in the countryside where the mountains come down to the plain of Lombardy, is more accentuated, but the head is still stamped with intelligence and spirit. Here is a man who did not boast of his birth, as Del Monte did.

In Bologna, the Council met in the city church of San Petronio. It was a very suitable setting for a truncated refugee assembly such as met in it, for the church of San Petronio in Bologna is one of the architectural tragedies of the West. In the year 1390, the Council of the Six Hundred decided to start building the city church that had so long been planned and to dedicate it to the city's patron saint, Petronius. In dimension and shape it was to outshine all churches of Italy. Antonio di Vicenzo, the architect, in collaboration with the beggar-monk Andrea da Faenza, designed a Gothic basilica with a three-aisled nave and also a three-aisled transept. The crossing was to be crowned with an octagonal cupola and the choir to have an ambulatorium. The plan provided for a structure 650 feet long and some 450 feet wide at the transept. The aisles of the nave were to have chapels off them, which would give the impression of a five-aisled structure. However, no more than the nave was built. This was finished except for the vaulting by 1440 and was given a provisional timber roof. Then began two centuries of tribulation, that only ended when Girolamo Rinaldi compromised and vaulted the central nave, leaving the other aisles as they were.

157, 158

When the Council Fathers met in Bologna, the nave still had its temporary timber roof, though part of the marble façade was complete. On this, Jacobo della Quercia, a sculptor who was said to be both a hundred years behind the times and a hundred years ahead of his day, has depicted the story of the seven days of creation. His Adam and Eve have the splendid physique one does not expect to see before the work of Michaelangelo a hundred years later, but they still have that fervent, pious zest for life that illumined the thirteenth and fourteenth centuries.

159–160

On April 24, 1547, Charles V did battle with the troops of the Schmalkaldian League of Protestant princes at Mühlberg on the Elbe, defeating them and taking their leader, Johann Friedrich, Elector of Saxony, prisoner. The imperial army was commanded by Charles V (1500–1558) in person. Titian has painted him as in the evening after the battle. Ever since they met in 1530 at the court of the Gonzaga in Mantua, Titian had been attached to the Emperor, whose lifelong friend and favourite painter he became, and by whom he was raised to the rank of baron and later to that of Count Palatine. After the battle of

Mühlberg, the Emperor sent for Titian to come to Augsburg. The court wished to have a portrait of the victor. Titian journeyed across the Alps in January 1548, but he did not meet the Emperor, who was suffering from gout, until April. It was then that he painted the famous portrait, now in the old Pinakotek in Munich, which shows the invalid Emperor sitting in an armchair, on a balcony, wearing his usual black costume and cap that he owed to his Spanish origins. On his right and behind him is a pillar of the gallery, and beyond you see meadows and trees with a low horizon. On the balustrade of the balcony is carved the date, 1548. It was from this portrait that Titian developed his great equestrian picture of the victor of Mühlberg, which depicts him riding out of a wood at evening, gazing vigorously and intently out over the valley of the Elbe. Charles loved the art of horsemanship and equestrian combat, an inheritance from Maximilian I, the last of the knights, and perhaps also from his Burgundian ancestors. He is riding a black Spanish horse, which has a matt red cover embroidered in gold. His gilded armour made by Desiderius Colman of Augsburg, reflects darts of light. His sash, like the horse-cover is red, the colour of victory, and this is repeated in the plume of his peaked helmet. In his right hand he holds a lance, which is intended to be a repetition of the spear which Caesar had when he crossed the Rubicon on his way to capture Rome. The colours are tinged with evening and the shadows are nestling in the folds in the ground and under the trees. The sunset is fighting against the clouds of night.

The Emperor rides past in the last light of day and does not see us. He is alone with his victory, which is that of a view of life. This is not a picture, for which "The Victor" would be a suitable title. Adolfo Venturi, the Italian art historian, has rightly compared it to Dürer's engraving "Knight, Death and Devil". Like it, Titian's portrait is also an allegory, presenting the concept of the Empire in the person and destiny of Charles V, whom he rightly saw as the chivalrous knight making a last attempt to reconstruct the Holy Roman Empire in a world grown hostile to it. The Emperor was the product of the German lands, but Italian artists made the concept of Empire immortal, both in Dante's great *Divine Comedy* and in this equestrian portrait that Titian painted three hundred years later, in which the unity of Europe became a triumphant fact, if only in art.

The battle of Mühlberg was fought three days after the Council held its first meeting in Bologna. Charles V thought that he had thereby saved the Council and took for granted that it would transfer back to Trent. This, however, Paul III opposed. In Germany, too, the victory at Mühlberg bore little fruit. At the Reichstag held in Augsburg in 1548, it was only under duress that the Protestants would promise to send representatives to the Council of Trent.

Paul III never forgave the Emperor for being involved in the murder of his son Pier Luigi Farnese. In Bologna, the Council issued not a single decree. It was not transferred back to Trent till May 1, 1551, the order for this being signed by a different Pope, Julius III (1550–1555), who had been legate to the previous Council as Cardinal Del Monte. He succeeded Paul III on the papal throne on February 7, 1550.

The new session in Trent opened hopefully. It re-enacted the doctrine of the Holy Eucharist, dealt with the Sacrament of penance and auricular confession and declared the Anointing of the sick to be a Sacrament. The fact that the German Protestants were participating also aroused great hopes. On October 11, 1551, the envoys of the Church of Brandenburg accepted the decisions of the Council. However, the envoys of Württemberg and of the Free City of Strassburg, who did not arrive till later, upheld the reservations made at the Augsburg Reichstag and insisted that the Council must not be under the leadership of the Pope, and that all decrees so far passed must be debated afresh. They also demanded that bishops be relieved of their oaths of fealty to the Pope and the Pope subordinate himself to the Council.

Negotiations over these debatable points had become bogged down and the efforts at union all but wrecked, when Maurice, Elector of Saxony, concluded an alliance with France and, in March 1552, began a new war against Charles V. In view of this additional, external danger, the Council decided, on April 28, 1552, to adjourn, and the Council Fathers returned to their dioceses. Pope Julius III tried to embody the results so far achieved in a reform bull, but he died before this could be issued. His successor, another papal legate at Trent, Cardinal Cervini, who became Pope Marcellus II, also died before any decisive steps could be taken.

On May 23, 1555 Pope Paul IV was elected, and on that occasion Cardinal Seripando said: "God grant that he will carry through the reforms of the Church that Paul III so wished for verbally. The latter talked and did nothing. Julius said nothing and did nothing, Marcellus did what he could and said nothing. If only Paul IV would speak and act—do what he says. . . ." Paul was of the noble Neapolitan family of the Carafa. He had been in Spain and England as papal legate, and, in 1542, with Saint Gaetano of Tiene had founded the reform order of the Theatines. Gian Pietro Carafa was a pure and ardent priest, but inconsiderate. As Pope, he expended his energies on passionate hatred of Charles V and Philip II of Spain; while in the church itself he made the Inquisition, which was the department for the investigation of heresies, a central institution. He is supposed to have been the author of that horrible oath: "If my own father were a heretic, I would collect the wood with which to burn him." He was just as unfortunate with the first index of forbidden books issued in 1557, for zealous priests like Saint Petrus Canisius, the first German Jesuit, regarded it as a stumbling-block. No wonder, then, that, when he died, the people of Rome set fire to the buildings of the Inquisition and overthrew the statue of him that had been erected on the Capitol.

His contemporaries condemned Paul IV as a hidebound ascetic, a man who knew neither love nor moderation, and as such he is represented in the seated marble figure on his tomb, which is in Santa Maria *163* sopra Minerva in Rome, in the Chapel of the Carafas. It was designed by Pirro Ligorio, who here went back to the wall-niche tomb of the ancients. The sarcophagus stands free by itself and above it, in a niche, sits the figure of the Pope. The tiara and the papal vestments seem far too big for his shrivelled old man's figure. They are as much too big for him, as the office was while he was alive. Even the gesture of the right hand raised in benediction seems formal and far-fetched. Seldom can a mediocre sculptor with a mediocre subject have succeeded so perfectly in portraying ability and destiny.

Towards the end of his life, Paul IV had turned definitely towards church reform. Here, however, his ideas were medieval: he wanted to put the reforms through at a new papal Council to be held in the Lateran, for which reason until he died he opposed the reopening of the Council of Trent. His successor, Pius IV thought differently and

faced with other difficulties. He was friendly, witty and yet a simple
man, even though he was a Medici, not however a member of the
princely Florentine family. He was born in Milan on March 31, 1499,
the son of a notary. In all church questions he went to work soberly and
with moderation, and thus succeeded in bringing the difficult Council
of Trent to a successful conclusion.

164   Bastiano Torrigiani made a bust of him, as he did of Popes Pius IV,
Gregory XIII and Sixtus V. These busts are all executed in the same
style—Torrigiani had the mannerist's fear of empty areas—and that of
Paul IV is one of the more important. Torrigiani has covered the papal
robes with reliefs. To the right and left of the cloak's clasp are Peter and
Paul the Apostles, framed in decorative foliage. The Pope's head is bent
forward, so that the light plays on the metal dome of his bald head. It is
a thoughtful face that the well-trimmed beard frames. Torrigiani
modelled it in wood, and even the bronze has acquired the immediacy
of life. This is the head of an old man who is composed and wise,
charitable and loving. It is filled with the ardour of faith and that love
of art, which found expression in the Pope's friendship with Michaelangelo, whom he commissioned to make the Church of Santa Maria
degli Angeli out of the Baths of Diocletian and to continue building
Saint Peter's.

In 1541, the reformer, John Calvin's State of God was set up in
Geneva. Calvin was a French priest. He became early acquainted with
Luther's teachings, but set up his own system of reforms in opposition to
him. One of his main points was predestination, i.e. that people's
destiny in time and eternity is determined beforehand by God. According to him, the righteous form a state of God already on earth. In 1540
an unknown artist painted Calvin as the distinguished humanist with a
white frilled collar half hidden by his full beard and a doctor's cap
165   elegantly tilted over his right ear. In his left hand, he holds the leather
gloves of the burgess. Calvin's character is perhaps, better depicted in a
later head-and-shoulder's portrait. This is dominated by the face.
Clothes are mere incidentals. The long, narrow face is dominated by its
huge nose; the eyes, cold and sceptical, lie deep-set, the lips are curled
disdainfully under the bushy beard. In this face there is none of that
Divine fire that lights the face of the young Luther in Lucas Cranach's
portrait. The difference between the doctrine and attitude of the two

reformers is well expressed in their portraits. In that of Calvin, we see the aspect of the power that was preparing to conquer the world and its newly discovered continent in the name of the God of the Old Testament. It is the face of an idealist, whose large eyes are gazing into a future which is our present, the age in which work is performed as a moral duty and in honour of God, and money and success are the visible signs of God's redemption. This is the view of life first propounded by John Calvin of Noyon. Though his French adherents were butchered in the blood bath of Vassy in 1562, his spirit permeated Western Euope and found itself a stronghold in North America.

Although Calvin set up his State of God in Geneva as early as 1541, Rome and the Council of Trent were so busy watching the reformation in Germany, that they remained unaware of Calvinism until it had already begun to spread in France. Pius IV then decided to recall the Council and this he did on November 29 1560. Any who had hoped that the Council, reassembled in Trent, would take steps against the Calvinists were soon disappointed. The Council had already defined the Church's views on the doctrines of the reformers, and its only concern now was to bring new forces to life in the Church itself and to carry through reforms. It sought to achieve the unity of Christendom; but now there was no Emperor to take its decisions and make them temporal law and to persecute all who resisted or opposed them.

The man who was Emperor in 1562 was neither a Constantine nor a Justinian. Hans Lautensack made an engraving of him, a man in *166* Spanish court dress looking in at a window that is overloaded with ornamentation in the style of German mannerism. In the background is the silhouette of the city of Vienna. The man looks worried and hesitant, gazing into the world of which Luther, in the last few years of his life, said that he would rather send for the hangman to come and send him out of it, than live another forty years in it. This Emperor is Ferdinand II (1503–1564), brother of Charles V who, in 1556, had withdrawn to the monastery of Geronimo de Juste in Spain, where he died in 1558. Charles was the last Emperor in the West, Ferdinand being more of a local ruler intent on the balance of power. In 1555 he made religious peace with the Protestant German princes at Augsburg.

Charles V had sought to influence the Council; but in its third and last session-period Ferdinand I did just as the Pope wished, and thus the

Council of Trent did finally become a Pope's Council and, under Pius IV, that favoured reform. In Cardinal Morone, Pius IV found a president who was a definite advocate of reform. He put through the measures that later became known as the Tridentine reforms. These were based on the principle that in everything it was the welfare of the soul that was decisive. The new decrees made it incumbent upon every diocese to have a seminar for priests. The official duties of cardinals and bishops were defined afresh, and care of souls was organized.

In 1619, Paolo Sarpi, first historian of the Council, wrote that the reforms of Trent were a myth, the Council a trick on the part of the Popes in order to seize power again. Was that why the Council was brought so quickly, perhaps precipitately, to an end? Was there some truth, perhaps, in the malicious French saying the Holy Ghost came to Trent in the wallets of the couriers from Rome? Was the Calvinist Languet right, when he wrote home that at Trent bishops sold their souls for little more than the German mercenaries their arms? You cannot help asking yourself this and other questions as you walk through the streets of Trento today. In the cathedral and Santa Maria Maggiore the places where the Council met have been preserved almost intact, and there are also paintings to show us them as they were then. These two buildings comprise the centre of Trento, which still has the same *167* layout of streets as that shown in a plan of 1580. New buildings have been put up, but between them still lie the Council's palaces, like precious caskets of memories.

In the cathedral square is Haus Rella, which, like all buildings used *168* by the Council, now has a plaque with the inscription *Città del Concilio*. Marcello Fogolino painted the frescoes on its façade. These show Apollo, Diana and Cupid in the blue horizon of a landscape such as may have existed before the Garden of Eden. The Palazzo Tonarelli displays the squared stone of the Renaissance, two sides of the Palazzo del Monte display the elegance of early mannerism in building; while the city's towers have the hard massiveness of the medieval fortified city. As a sort of go-between there is the Castello standing between them and the *169* friendlily open palaces. It is called Buon Consiglio, Good Advice, and Dürer made it the subject of one of the water-colours he brought back from his first journey in Italy, and he took it for the model of one of his first independent architectural pictures. The Castello stands on the site of the camp of the old Roman legion. It is medieval, part Renaissance and part Baroque, as is its sculpture, and it is in a way a marriage of the forms and ideas of North and South.

Was all that was done in vain? Again we see how even eyewitnesses of historical events can be mistaken. Who knew what would be the result of the proposals, votes, enthusiasm or irritation, when the Council Fathers walked through the streets of Trent, discussing the last session, God and the world with their fellows? The Council was a great gamble. It not only exceeded all the others in duration and number of those who attended it; but never before had the Church discussed so many things or so topically; never before had the Church thought so profoundly and pithily. No other Council had so greatly influenced the following centuries or injected the church with such enduring vigour.

That is the judgment of ecclesiastical historians today, and it is confirmed by the wealth of art to which the Council gave rise. It is the work of the best painters of the sixteenth century Raphael and Titian. It covers five Popes: Paul III in Raphael's family group, and in the monument in Saint Peter's that dello Porta put up to him; Julius III in Pulzone's one picture in the Galleria Spada; Marcellus II in Salviati's statue; Paul IV in the statue over his tomb in Santa Maria Minerva and Pius IV in Torrigiani's bust of him now in London. There is Charles V riding into immortality in the guise that Titian gave him, the last knight to be Holy Roman Emperor. There is Cranach's portrait of the ardent young Luther, the Old Testamentary zeal of Calvin in the unknown artist's portrait of him. Cardinal Madruzzo comes to life again to live for ever as Titian's youthful prince of the Church.

It would be strange, if a Council that gave rise to such art, had not concerned itself with Art; and, indeed, among the many decrees issued on December 3 and 4 in its twenty-fifth and last session, there is one concerned with "The Invocation and Veneration of Relics of Saints and of Images of Saints." It is not out of place among all the other decrees dealing with the welfare of the soul and with the Sacraments; for they were not without their influence on these works of art that have triumphed over forgetfulness.

This was the occasion of the second picture-storm that swept Christendom. The reformers were very Old Testament-minded and the absolute prohibition of images of the Maccabean age appealed to their strict zeal, and when this conflicted with the store of treasures built up during the late Middle Ages—it resulted in a sort of spiritual short circuit. Supposing the many pictures of Christ, the Virgin Mary and the Saints to be the expression of a new idolatry, they stormed the churches and destroyed and burned paintings and statues. Countless works of art were lost in this wave of iconoclasm; many districts lost every example of Medieval art they had. Martin Luther may have raised his voice against cruel, ruthless tyrants, the Calvinists and Hussites refused the religious pictures any right to exist. The walls of Europe's churches became bare.

That is why the West expected some pronouncement from the Council of Trent in this question of pictures. The decree provided this. Pictures of Christ, the Virgin Mary and the Saints were due honour and veneration, not because anyone believed that they possessed Divine essence or power, nor because they could be petitioned for things or that one could put one's trust in them, that was only done among peoples who placed their hopes in idols. Pictures could be venerated, because the honour shown to them was really paid to the being they depicted. When you kiss a picture, bow to it or kneel before it, you are worshipping Christ and honouring the Saints.

There was nothing new here, as the Council Fathers knew: this was just what the Second Council of Nicaea had decreed concerning the iconoclasts of Byzantium. But there are ideas that have to be restated every so often. The Tridentine decree on pictures and images appeared at the right moment. It encouraged bishops and princes, abbots and priests to give artists new commissions and it gave painters and sculptors the freedom, which was to give rise to the magnificent work of the age of Baroque.

THE VATICAN

TO the right of the Porta Pia in Rome is an expanse of marble
wall with solemn inscriptions that shines whitely in the red of the   *170*
brickwork of the city wall of Rome. Those who pass by along
Corso d'Italia scarcely notice it and few know what the wording on it
has to tell, yet it has an important message and marks a place of considerable historical importance. It was here that, on September 20,
1870, the Papal State came to an end, it was here that the twentieth
general assembly, the First Vatican Council broke up.

On September 2, 1870, Napoleon III's French Empire was smashed
at the Battle of Sedan. The Papal State thereby lost its strongest ally,
and Garibaldi, the eternal revolutionary of the Risorgimento, prepared
to march on Rome. The Government of Victor Emmanuel II, wanted
to get in ahead of him, and, on September 20, its troops shot a breach
in the city wall near the Porta Pia, and, within a few hours, the city,
which put up scarcely any defence, was in their hands. That was the
end of the Pope's secular sovereignty. Italy was united within her
natural boundaries. This stormy day also ended the Twentieth Ecumenical Council, which had been meeting in the Vatican since
December 8, 1869. It is this breach in the walls, through which the
king of Italy's troops entered Rome, that the marble memorial in
Corso d'Italia now fills.

In 1870, photography had not yet ousted the woodcut or the litho-
graph, which till then had provided topical pictures, and it is a woodcut that has immortalized the entry of the Italian army through the   *171*
Porta Pia, which was speedily opened. It depicts infantry and baggage-
wagons making for the gate that stands majestically open. Michaelangelo designed the Porta Pia in 1561, as a single Roman triumphal   *172*
arch, and it was as a triumphal arch that it was used on September 20.
Those with a sense for historical contrasts will enjoy this woodcut.
Pius IV, the last Pope of the Council of Trent, had the Porta Pia built,

and it resulted in the break-up of the next Ecumenical Council. The Pope of this First Vatican Council, another Pius, lost the Papal State to one of the successors of the last anti-popes in history, the Duke Amadeus of Savoy, whom the Council of Basle made Pope as Felix V.

The five of the nineteen Councils that had preceded that of the Vatican were held in Rome, always in the Lateran. Pius IX broke this tradition and had his Council meet in Saint Peter's in the Vatican. This new site was of as great historical importance as any of the previous ones. Since the Third Council of Constantinople, which met in Hagia Sophia, none had had a setting that could compare with Saint Peter's.

In ancient Rome, the Vatican lay outside the gates. It contained the tomb of the Emperor Hadrian, which later became the Castel Sant' Angelo. The site of Saint Peter's was one of the city's largest cemeteries, and Nero's circus probably lay to the left of it. The Emperor's garden lay along the slopes of the nearby Gianicolo. It was in Circus Nero that Saint Peter the Apostle suffered a martyr's death in the year A.D. 67, 65 or 66 and was buried in the nearby heathen burial ground. On the site of this cemetery the Emperor Constantine built one of his great churches about the year 324, choosing not the level ground at the bottom, nor the top of the hill, but the actual steep hillside, along which ran a path through the graves. Because of this the southern walls of the nave and transept had to be built on substructures, often as much as forty feet high. The resulting empty space was filled in with earth. At the same time the side of the hill had to be cut away in order to provide a level area. It was a tremendous undertaking and one can only see the sense of it, if one believes the tradition that Constantine had the altar of this church sited over the untouched grave of Saint Peter. Archaeological research has confirmed this within recent years.

Constantine's basilica, which Silvester I, Pope of the First Council of Nicaea, consecrated on November 18, 326, was a five-aisled structure. To the west, it had a mighty transept, which the apse joined. To the east, facing the city, was a great atrium, and the open court with its fountain was enclosed by cloisters.

173–175
177–179 In 1452, they began replacing the delapidated structure of Constantine's basilica with a new church. The best architects of the Renaissance and Baroque were employed on it. Bramante designed a three-aisled structure with the ground plan of a Greek cross. A huge dome

was to rise over its crossing. Bramante wanted to combine the style of two of ancient Rome's buildings, the Pantheon and Constantine's basilica. Raphael rejected this idea. He wanted a three-aisled, longitudinal basilica. Michaelangelo reverted to Bramante's original idea, simplified it and built it as far as the drum of the cupola with its windows. His successor completed the magnificent twin bowl of the dome, heightening it and extending it. The structure of the new church, completed in 1590, had the ground plan of a Greek cross and covered only part of the area of the former building. Its interior with the emphasis on the middle ran counter to the established form of Western ecclesiastical architecture, which had preferred the Latin cross. The demands on divine service made after the Council of Trent required an interior that led, straight and severe as a street, to the high altar, as was the traditional way. That is why Pope Paul V went back to the plan of a long structure and commissioned Carlo Maderna to extend the church to the east. Work began in 1607 and the addition was consecrated in 1626. Gian Lorenzo Bernini who took charge of the work after Maderna, finished Saint Peter's in the years 1656–1667 with the splendid Outer Court of Saint Peter's Square. Inside, Saint Peter's has become a three-aisled basilica. It had a transept, and the great dome towered over the crossing. The dimensions are huge: 694 feet long, 376 feet wide (499 feet at the transepts) and 405 feet high, to the top of the dome. The naves are barrel-vaulted. The neat interior is graced with ornamentation, sculpture and paintings, accentuated with altars and tombs; yet for all its size it is human. Beneath the dome, in the centre of this vast interior, lies Peter the Apostle, the papal altar rising over his grave.

Great and many-sided though the Council of Trent was, and though it lent spirit and life to a whole epoch, like all that is human, it was not perfect. It neglected the tenets of the Church. The later Popes and their architects seem to have wished to complete architecturally what it had left undone. When Bernini built his colonnades round Saint Peter's Square, the Pope's church achieved great unity of form and concept; yet it was to be centuries before the Church gave similar unity to its theological structure.

Saint Peter's Square is no ordinary square. Its colonnades are like avenues of stone, and the obelisque gives it a calm centre. Two fountains cast sparkling lights into space. The whole is aimed at the façade to which Maderna gave strong, shadow-building articulation. The central part has, at ground level, three rectangular and two round-arched doorways; they are separated by immense Corinthian columns. Above the central doorway is the benediction balcony, from which, on special occasions, the Pope gives his blessing *urbi et orbi*, and from which on the election of a new Pope, the deacon of the College of Cardinals announces his name.

On December 8, 1869, Pope Pius IX proclaimed the Twentieth General Council open from this balcony. Saint Peter's Square has witnessed many great occasions and this was one of them. It is recorded 176 in a new kind of picture, which shows a white awning stretched above the balcony. The back of the square is occupied by papal soldiers and the Pope's Swiss guard, and in the foreground are countless cabs with hoods up, all facing the front of Saint Peter's. It is a photograph.

From the First to the Nineteenth Council, means of transport remained the same: the Council Fathers reached their destinations either on foot, or horseback, in a hores-drawn carriage or sailing ship; to the Twentieth Council, however, they came by train or steamer. News of the doings of the first nineteen councils was disseminated by by letter or messenger, that of the Twentieth Council by telegraph, while the Press circulated its debates in a way hitherto unknown. The pictures of the first nineteen councils are from the hand of painters and sculptors, but with the Twentieth Council they had to compete with the photographers. This photograph of the proclamation of the Vatican Council is the first Council photograph.

After the opening session, Bishop Ullathorne of Birmingham said that the world had never before witnessed such an assembly of prelates, either in their numbers or in the nature of their training and experience. Out of the 1,050 bishops of the Church, 774 were assembled in Rome. The Council met in the right-hand part of the transept of Saint Peter's. 181 An anonymous artist shows the order of seating. Those entitled to vote sit in eight rows one behind the other; below them the officials and stenographers have their places. Above the rows of the Council Fathers are the tribunes for advisory theologians and guests of honour. A Council altar has been set up to one side of the papal altar. Opposite it, in the main semicircular wall of the transept is the seat of the president.

Michaelangelo's great design with its columns and pilasters beneath massive barrel-vaulting makes an unique architectural frame for the Council.

Pius IX, Pope of the First Vatican Council, was born on May 13, 1792 in Sinigaglia, as Giovanni Maria Count Mattai-Feretti. When he mounted Saint Peter's throne in 1846, the hopes of an Italy that was striving for civic liberty and unity were centred on him. However, the events of 1848 turned the disappointed Pope into an unyielding advocate of absolution. There is a photograph of this Pius IX, sitting surrounded by his cabinet, rather as Raphael depicted old Paul III with his relatives. This early photograph reveals an uncanny possibility for even *182* a photograph to reveal the background of personalities and their relations. Here is an interesting collection of human passions with Pius IX in the middle, a gracious, but hidebound prince of the Papal State. "I am the stone. Where I fall, there I lie," he said of himself. Another, later, photograph shows the Pope alone at his desk above which is a crucifix. This is the Pope who, in 1854, proclaimed the dogma of the Immaculate Conception, introduced the feast of the Sacred Heart in 1856, and, in 1864 enquired of the cardinals whether they did not think that "the exceptional distress of the Church could be remedied by the exceptional means of a Council."

No other Council had been so well prepared in advance as that now held in the Vatican. The subjects to be discussed were laid down beforehand. Five sub-committees debated them. They were Dogma, Church Discipline, the Orders, the Eastern Church and Missions and, lastly, Church Policy. The Council was thus able to set about discussing them at once, the spadework having been already done. The world waited tensely. Pius IX had already caused a stir with his *syllabus* of 1864, which condemned the philosophical system of Rationalism, Pantheism, false political ideas like Communism and unchristian ideas in morality, wedlock and the State. Interest became feverish when the Jesuit periodical *Civilta Cattolica* in its issue of February 6, 1869, stated that in all probability the coming Council would proclaim the infallibility of the Pope. Certain European governments were alarmed by the idea. Prince Hohenlohe, prime minister of Bavaria, suggested that his and other governments should take joint steps to stop the plan. Bismarck was more clear-sighted. He wrote to the Prussian ambassador in Rome: "Participation by States in a Council could only be on a thoroughly foreign base which, where we are concerned, no longer exists, a relationship between State and Church that is now a thing of the past."

The Council issued a number of important decrees, before it came to this question of infallibility: the decree on faith dealt with the existence and recognition of a personal God, the necessity of Divine revelation, the character of faith and the relation between it and learning. Ministration was also dealt with. The primacy of the Pope was reaffirmed. Then, on July 11, 1870, the debate on the infallibility of the Pope began. No other decision by a Council can have been so discussed and misunderstood as this one. Any who think that the Council Fathers just tamely accepted drafts prepared by the sub-committees know little of these Councils. The debates on this question of infallibility were in no way different to the stormy sessions of parliaments today. It was strongly opposed, passionate speeches were made both for and against; and then, on July 14, it was approved. Of the Council Fathers present 533 voted for it and two voted against; most of its opponents had absented themselves from that session. The decree says that when the Pope in Rome makes a pronouncement *ex catedra*, that is when he is acting in his capacity as shepherd and teacher of all Christians, and by virtue of his supreme apostolic authority makes a final decision that a doctrine concerning faith or morals is to be held by the whole Church, he, by virtue of the Divine aid promised him in Saint Peter "possesses that infallibility with which the Divine Saviour wished to have His Church furnished for the definition and doctrine concerning faith or morals; and that such definitions of the Roman pontiff are of themselves, not in consequence of the Church's consent, irreformable".

After this memorable session the Vatican Council adjourned. When Rome capitulated on September 20, 1870, and Pius IX began his symbolical resistance to the kingdom of Italy as "the prisoner in the Vatican," there was no more question of continuing the Council. Formally, it has never been concluded; but legally it came to an end when Pope John XXIII convoked the Second Vatican Council on Christmas Day 1961.

A dreadful thunderstorm raged over the Vatican during the last session of the Council that never ended. According to eyewitnesses it

183

was quite dark in Saint Peter's and the candles were lit. G. Altobelli, who painted the scene, did not know how to deal with this and has *180* sunlight pouring in through the right of the transept. The scene is as viewed from a tribune on the right-hand long wall. Altobelli has reproduced the architecture, statuary and paintings in accurate detail, even more accurate are the faces and, indeed, if you examine the picture, you will see that the interior and robes are painted, but the faces have been taken from photographs and stuck on to the canvas. Thus the painter and the photographer have here joined forces. The photographers of the 1870's, of course, did not have wide-angle lenses and could not have taken the whole Council from the point from which this picture was painted. Only the painter could do that.

Altobelli's picture is the strangest of all the Council documents. Judged by its artistic merits it should be on the nineteenth-century scrap-heap, but it is a document both of the Council and of a surrender, the artist's surrender to the photographer of his highest documentary task, that of depicting the human countenance.

When the city wall was breached and Rome taken, many contemporaries thought that the end of the Roman Catholic Church was at hand. The Pope had lost his secular arm; while his spiritual one seemed paralysed by this new dogma of his infallibility. The Council that never ended had not succeeded in settling the tenets of the Church for which people had hoped ever since Trent.

Painting, of course, did not die with the advent of photography. What looked like an end was also a beginning, and by conceding to photography its traditional task of reportage, painting won a freedom of creation that led to new forms and new expressions. Nor was the Roman Church anywhere near the end of its history. What had looked like the end was again, perhaps, a new beginning. The Pope was relieved of the burden of temporal power. The lack of definition of the Church gave him freedom to make the Church effective in new areas and in the altered situation of the secularized west. The decrees of the Vatican Council on the primacy and infallibility of the Pope did not hamper Pius IX's successors, but rather helped them to gain authority even outside the Church of Rome.

The First Vatican Council was wrecked on the struggle between Italy and the Vatican; when the Second Council was opened on

October 11, 1962, the President of Italy sat in the chief seat of the guests of honour beneath the great dome of Saint Peter's. The reconciliation between Italy and the Vatican, begun with the Lateran Treaty of 1927, was complete. When the First Vatican Council met, a few governments of Europe wondered whether they ought not to intervene. On October 11, 1962 no government in the world even considered such a step, and all states of the free world sent delegations to the opening. They came from not only Europe, America and Australia, but the states of Africa and Asia were also independently represented. When Pius IX invited the other Christian Churches to the first Vatican Council, he received bitter refusals. John XXIII did not let himself be put off by this, and, this time, many of the other Christian Churches sent observers, who had the right to attend any session of the Council.

This catholic, i.e. all-embracing relationship of the Church to the world was observable in the procession of Council Fathers that crossed Saint Peter's Square on the morning of the opening day. The bishops *185* and patriarchs of the oriental Churches wore their crowns with the same authority as their western brethren their white mitres; the black cardinals joined in the procession that was 2,000 strong, as naturally as the white. This remained the central spiritual phenomenon of the first series of meetings which ended on December 8, 1962. Bishops got to know the problems of other countries and continents through personal contact with their delegates; the European discovered that Negroes, Chinese and Japanese were indeed his equals and able to maintain their views in opposition to his. The world church had become a reality.

In the Second Vatican Council some 2,700 were entitled to attend and to vote. They are too many to be accommodated in the right arm *188* of the transept, in fact the central nave is scarcely large enough for them. This was the splendid aula in which, on September 29, 1963, the *186* Fathers met to start the second session. Here, too, they debated in the *187* presence of the Gospel which, as in all Councils, lay in a place of honour in the midst of the assembly. For the occasion, one of the most precious manuscripts of the Renaissance was chosen, that prepared at Ferrara between 1478–1482.

When Pope John XXIII died on June 3, 1962, many people thought that this would endanger the Council; but his successor, Paul VI,

Cardinal Archbishop Giovanni Montini of Milan, had no hesitation in *189* continuing the great work. In the intervening period, the various committees continued their work, so that the by time the second session began, there were seventeen drafts awaiting the Council. These were entitled: Divine Revelation, The Church, The Blessed Virgin Mary; Bishops and the Administration of Dioceses; Ecumenism, The Clergy; the Members of Orders; Lay Apostles; The United Churches of the East; the Holy Liturgy; Ministration; The Sacrament of Marriage; the Training of Clergy; Catholic Schools and Universities; Missions; Mass Media (Press, Wireless, Film and Television).